Dan,

Happy 50th! I hope this helps to bag the big one! I love you,

Cyndi

THE COMPLETE HUNTER™

ULTIMATE ELK
HUNTING

Strategies, Techniques & Methods

Jay Houston

Creative Publishing
international

Minneapolis, Minnesota

Jay Houston is a nationally requested conference speaker, editor, publisher, hunting consultant, and big game hunter. He is also the founder of The Outfitter Network and ElkCamp.com, America's leading online resource of information for elk hunters. As a freelance writer for more than 20 years, Jay has authored and published numerous books, articles and stories on a variety of outdoor topics. Jay lives in Missouri with his wife Rae Ann.

Dedication

This book is dedicated to the men and women, staff and volunteers of the Rocky Mountain Elk Foundation and to the hundreds of thousands of elk hunters and outdoorsmen who have faithfully supported this great organization in its mission to preserve elk and elk country. Without the ceaseless efforts of RMEF and other organizations like it, we would not be able to honestly say, "These are the good old days."

Acknowledgments

This volume would not have been possible without the generous contributions of some great photographers: Jerry Taylor, Jim Christensen, Jerry Gowins, Jr., Brad Knutson, Andrew Bracken and Jeff McKinney.

Creative Publishing international

Creative Publishing international, Inc.
400 First Avenue North
Suite 300
Minneapolis, MN 55401
1-800-328-3895
www.creativepub.com
All rights reserved

Printed in China

10 9 8 7 6 5 4 3 2 1

Library of Congress Cataloging-in-Publication Data
Houston, Jay
 Ultimate elk hunting : strategies for today's hunter / Jay Houston.
 p. cm.
Includes index.
 ISBN-13: 978-1-58923-353-9 (hard cover)
 ISBN-10: 1-58923-353-0 (hard cover)
 1. Elk hunting. I. Title.
SK303.H68 2008
799.2'76542--dc22   2007033717

President/CEO: Ken Fund
VP for Sales & Marketing: Kevin Hamric
Publisher: Bryan Trandem
Acquisitions Editor: Barbara Harold
Production Managers: Laura Hokkanen, Linda Halls
Creative Director: Michele Lanci-Altomare
Senior Design Managers: Jon Simpson, Brad Springer
Design Managers: Sara Holle, James Kegley
Book & Cover Design: Danielle Smith
Page Layout: Danielle Smith

Text © 2008 Jay Houston

CONTENTS

INTRODUCTION

Ask just about any hunter what he or she considers to be the pinnacle of big game hunting in North America and most will say without hesitation the majestic bull elk, or wapiti (pronounced waapeetee). They inhabit the dark timber forests of the Canadian Rockies, Oregon, Washington and Idaho, southward to the aspen groves and high country bowls of Colorado, Utah, Wyoming and Montana, to the arid high desert country of Nevada, New Mexico and Arizona, and even limited coastal ranges in California. These elusive tawny-colored, thick-antlered brutes—with heavy odorous dark manes and facial features—may tip the scales at over a thousand pounds (453 kg), are the stuff that a big game hunter's dreams are made of.

While those of us who live and work in elk country definitely contribute to the overall numbers of elk hunters who head out each fall for those secret high-mountain hidey-holes, the majority of elk hunters do not live in elk country. Rather, they are deer hunters and turkey hunters from the Midwest, Northeast, South and all areas in between, seeking to bag that trophy of a lifetime. So what is it that draws hundreds of thousands of hunters westward each fall in search of these elusive ghosts of the high country?

Having pursued these magnificent creatures and sat around many a high country campfire for nearly 20 years, I know of four basic reasons why most hunters answer the call of elk country. First, they want to experience the majesty of how vast and truly wild this country can be. Like so many who journey westward each year, I grew up hunting whitetail deer with my dad and brother in hardwood forests and farm country back east. I honestly never took the time to think about the size of the areas we used to hunt, but if my memory serves me, some of those woodlots may have been 20 or 30 acres (8 or 12 ha) and the farms perhaps 200 acres (80 ha). These seemed fairly large to a fourteen-year-old. A relatively small piece of elk country tucked away in the corner of a county in any elk hunting state, on the other hand, is often measured in hundreds of thousands of square acres (ha), where a lone hunter can stand on a precipice and see 100 miles (161 km) in almost any direction, perhaps even into the next state.

The second reason hunters come to elk country is the challenge of conquering this big land, surviving the extremes in weather and besting the beast on his own ground. Elk hunting is hard work. Long days are the rule, often requiring the hunter to rise in the wee hours far before dawn and not return to camp until long after the sun has disappeared behind the ridgeline to the west. Elk country is big country and effectively hunting it may mean hiking as many as 12 miles (19 km) in a single day. This isn't flat land hiking either. If you find yourself on level ground for more than half an hour during your trek, you are probably giving your hunt less than 100 percent effort.

The weather in elk country is finicky as well. Regardless of which state you may be hunting in, the weather has been known to go from subfreezing temps and clear skies before dawn to balmy temps in the 70s°F (20s°C) during midday; it can be clear one minute and then dark and ominous with snow or even lightning at the drop of a hat. Besting the beast often means dealing with a range of environmental challenges.

The third reason hunters come to elk country is in search of the massive racks that bull elk sport. Antlers are the crowning glory of a mature bull elk. They progressively increase in length and mass from his first year until around his seventh or eighth year, after which the rack begins to decline as the bull's ability to acquire the proper nutrition for good antler growth is reduced, usually due to age.

Trophy antlers are a prize to be cherished. They serve as a fond reminder of any hunt.

Finally, hunters come to elk country to experience the spine-tingling cacophony that occurs prior to and during the rut—the bugle of a bull elk. In over forty years of big game hunting across America, I have never experienced any sound in nature that will so stir the souls of hunters like the midnight or predawn serenade of a bull bugling to his cows. There is no other sound quite like it.

One of the aspects of our camp that really makes it something to look forward to is that everyone is more than willing to share their knowledge and experience with other members of camp, especially younger hunters. As experienced hunters, we have an obligation to pass along the lessons that we have learned, whether to the less experienced hunters in our camps or to those who are new to elk hunting. Years ago, I hunted in a few camps where it was an "every man for himself" atmosphere. To say the least, these were not camps that I would consider returning to. Elk hunting is as much about camaraderie as it is about bringing game to ground. Fireside stories and chats and brotherly banter in the cook tent over a cup of coffee or hot chocolate make up a large part of elk camp.

So grab a mug, sit down and read about the lessons, mishaps and joys of elk hunting that I'm about to share.

Once you hear an elk bugle in the wild, you'll want to hear it again and again.

Chapter 1

PLANNING YOUR HUNT

Years ago I learned the following motto and it is my absolute best tip: Prior Preparation Prevents Poor Performance. There are many things you can do to be prepared. If I had to choose one reason that I believe causes hunters to fall short in their pursuit of wapiti, I would have to say that far too many hunters do not invest enough time in planning their hunt.

Some time ago a wise fellow told me, "We get out of life what we put into it." It's not a difficult stretch to apply this wisdom to elk hunting.

The more time we spend investigating things—where to hunt, how to hunt and navigate that area, locating food and water sources, discovering travel and escape routes, understanding elk feeding behavior and so on—the more likely we are to find ourselves in the position to take a shot at that bull of a lifetime.

GETTING INTO SHAPE

How much effort do you need to put into getting into shape? Think of it as trying out for the high school football team; only those in the best of shape will be able to survive, much less achieve their objective of becoming a starting player. The good news is that day one of your preparation is the toughest. Every day of preparation thereafter, while by no means easy, will be less challenging than the day before as your mind and body get in shape.

You may ask, "I'm young (maybe 40) and in pretty good shape already; why should I have to put in this much effort?" Try this: Locate the biggest hill in your area, unless you live in Tibet; load up a day pack with say, a light load of 20 pounds (9 kg) of rocks, and try hiking up and down that hill four or five times. This is roughly the workout you will get before noon on opening day of elk season. Now how "in shape" do you feel? Get my point?

Sure footing and a pack that you can handle are just two important things to think about when in elk country.

Take advantage of anything that helps you cover more area—glassing from a high vantage point is one of them.

Less Oxygen Means More Work for Your Body

Here is something to consider about hunting at altitude. My former home in Colorado Springs is pretty much the lowland for Colorado, at approximately 7,000 feet (2,133 m) above sea level. In "The Springs," the amount of oxygen available to breathe is about 25 percent less than that available at sea level, as in most parts of Texas. Elk range is typically found at relatively high altitudes—roughly 6,000 to 12,500 feet (1,830 to 3,800 km)—compared to sea level. Basic high school science taught us that as we ascend in altitude, the amount of available oxygen decreases, that is, the higher you go, the less oxygen you have to breathe. Back when I was flying in the Air Force, we learned that there is something called a "standard lapse rate." Standard lapse rate says that in addition to some other things, as you ascend in altitude the amount of available oxygen decreases at a fixed rate.

Planning for a successful elk hunt in higher altitude areas like the Rockies, then, means understanding how the lower oxygen levels adversely affect the body.

Before I begin to tell you about all the negative effects of hunting at higher altitudes, I will offer one word of encouragement for those who, despite their best efforts, will find the lack of oxygen slowing them down. As I have gotten older, I have slowed down quite a bit as I move throughout elk country. A welcomed benefit of this new pace is I see more elk.

If you want to maximize your potential for a successful elk hunt, you need to figure out how you are going to prepare for and deal with having less oxygen to keep you going from long before sunrise to sunset, and maybe after. Your ability to effectively hunt in higher altitudes will be key to your success. Should you choose to disregard this key issue, it may play a deciding role in your failure to locate elk. The following are three key

Thrashing saplings and brush is part of a bull's routine breeding behavior. He deposits scent, an expression of dominance and marking territory.

factors that hunters who don't live or work at higher altitudes should integrate into their planning for a successful elk hunt. For those of you who do live at or above 5,000 feet (1,524 m), now would be a good time to take a break, stretch your legs and get a cup of coffee.

Build a plan that will prepare your body, specifically your lungs and cardiovascular system, for working longer and harder with less oxygen. In other words, do your homework.

Jay's Tip

Much of your success in elk hunting depends on (1) getting into good physical shape, and (2) spending plenty of pre-season time learning and scouting the ground you intend to hunt. Take it from one who has been there, most elk country is big and tough and will promptly kick your backside if you are not mentally and physically prepared to deal with it.

Don't make the mistake of so many who have come before you by thinking that you can wait until August and then begin taking leisurely strolls around the block or the park, and expect to get in shape. Such a workout regimen would probably prepare you for being the camp cook, but I can assure you, it will fall far short of preparing your lungs for what can realistically be a 14- to 20-hour day of humping up and down mountains with a rifle or bow and whatever other gear you carry. I suggest that you begin with a light cardio workout and then gradually increase the length and difficulty of your workout. This can be running, power walking, or jogging on the treadmill. In my opinion, for those who can afford one, a treadmill is the ultimate cardio trainer, especially those that can be programmed to simulate an uphill grade. These will vary your workout in speed and angle, which will help strengthen not only your cardiovascular system, but also those oh-so-important thigh, calf and ankle muscles, which are critical for endurance in hunting the Rockies. Treadmills also have the added value of making your workout weather-proof—you can maintain your workout schedule regardless of the weather.

OK, so now we have a written schedule for getting in shape. When should you begin? My answer is an emphatic now! I assume you are not reading this the week before elk season kicks off, but if you are, get off your backside and take this book for a long walk today! Really, each individual requires a different level of preparation, but on average, I suggest the following.

Begin your training a minimum of three months prior to your planned hunt date.

If you are what a personal trainer would say is in good or better cardiovascular shape, if you are well within the median of your weight range for your height and age, you may be able to reduce this lead time. As I am not a professional trainer, I strongly suggest that you consult your personal physician before beginning any type of exercise or workout program.

Finally, you should work diligently to ensure that your training program closely simulates what you expect to encounter in the real world.

While hunting, you will be carrying your day gear—food, survival gear, water, extra socks, and so on—in some type of pack. It is not important whether you choose a backpack or a fanny pack. Either will add extra weight that you will have to deal with during your hunt and you should train for this appropriately. I suggest beginning your training program by putting a few books in the pack and then continue to add more books as you train so that by the time you head off to camp, the weight of your pack actually exceeds that weight you expect to carry on your hunt. That way, when you head out into the boonies, not only will your cardiovascular system be ready, but so will your back and neck muscles.

No terrain seems too difficult for elk to maneuver. If you're to have success, you must take the same attitude.

PRE-SEASON PLANNING

When I was in school, I hated homework. Elk hunting homework is not so different, with one very important exception, the practical aspect. If you don't do your homework, your chances of locating elk in the millions of square miles (km) of wilderness are about as good as your chances of your boss saying "Why don't you take a few weeks off on me to go elk hunting?" Possible yes; probable, I don't think so. The practical advantage to doing your homework is the assurance that you are as prepared as possible for a successful elk hunt.

In my opinion a successful elk hunt is roughly 15 percent hunting skill, 15 percent luck and 70 percent first-class preparation. If you don't take time to prepare or if you cheat on this aspect of your hunt, don't be surprised when you go home empty-handed.

How much prep is enough? On average I spend about 10 hours of preparation throughout the year for every 1 hour actually hunting during elk season. If you figure that I hunt roughly 15 hours per day for 5 days—75 hours of hunting—my preparation for the hunt is around 750 hours spread throughout the year. Yeah, that is a lot of work!

When do I start planning my hunt? Each year my elk hunting homework begins not long after the previous season's end. For those of you who like to take notes, here is my four-step homework plan.

Step #1: Explore the Lessons That You Learned on the Previous Year's Hunt.

What worked and what didn't? I try to review every moment of that hunt, from the time we got out in the boonies (woods), to the elevations we hunted, wind direction and speed at various times of the day, time spent sitting and glassing versus time on the move, etc. You know the list. The difference is that I want to remember to repeat those activities that worked and dump or change those that failed to help bring an elk to ground. Why repeat something year after year that doesn't work?

High country bowls, especially those below a saddle, often hold elk.

Small, secluded park-like areas can provide elk with cover and a source of food.

Step #2: Determine If You Will Hunt the Same Area the Following Year or If You Need to Move to Another Area.

Let me clarify a point here. I hunt public land most of the time for a number of reasons, primarily because I cannot afford to drop $2,500-$5,000 per season to gain access to private land. Many of those trophy-size bulls you see in the magazines are found on private ranches, while the majority of Colorado's nearly 300,000 head of elk live most of their lives on public land, such as national forests, Bureau of Land Management land, or state land. Here are some good reasons to consider changing hunting areas: no elk or small numbers of elk in your area, very difficult or inaccessible terrain, or too many orange vests.

A UNIQUE STRATEGY

For years I hunted the same area in Routt County, Colorado. The area we hunted had two heavily used access points. Each morning we were all up and heading to our favorite benches, ridges and holes well before sunrise and every morning for years, a hunter would beat me to what I thought was a great stand. The guys in our camp had talked about it briefly the first year, but after that, every time I saw her orange vest sitting behind that blown-down aspen, I would be courteous and head off in another direction. At first I thought nothing of it, but eventually my curiosity got the better of me: just how did she manage to beat me to this spot regardless of how early I got there year after year? I determined to pay her a call to say hi the following season.

On opening day of the second combined rifle season, I headed out to make this visit. It was still darker than midnight but as I rounded the bend in the old logging road, I immediately saw she was waiting on me as if we had scheduled this rendezvous. I casually strolled over to her, making certain to let her know I was coming, to avoid getting shot. Imagine my surprise to discover that my friend was now only an orange vest draped carefully over a stump, presumably strategically placed there by someone to give hunters like me the impression of another hunter. Pretty smart, huh?

How do you determine if one area is better than another? To answer this question, you have to become somewhat of a detective. What you are looking for is information, the most valuable commodity on the planet. So don't expect to get it without making a personal investment. Keep in mind that anything of value doesn't come cheap.

Some good resources to start with are fellow hunters, Division of Wildlife or DNR officers, Forest Service rangers, landowners and the Internet. One thing to keep in mind when you want to strike up a conversation with any of the above, "when in Rome . . ." If you want to initiate a two-way dialogue with someone, particularly a dialogue where you expect that person to provide you with information, you need to make them feel comfortable talking with you. Be one of the boys. Leave the $400 cowboy boots and dude clothing at home, and avoid talking about "what you think" since most people, except those closest to you, don't really care what you think anyhow. Everyone, and I mean everyone, sooner or later likes to talk about themselves, so let them, while casually steering the conversation in the direction you would like it to go, specifically toward elk hunting.

A good GPS and topographical map are essentials in elk country.

Jay's Tip

Eighty percent of public land hunters hunt within 1 mile (1.6 km) of a road. Why? Because they are either lazy, physically limited or afraid of getting lost. Here's a hint: elk are not stupid and know to avoid these congested areas during hunting season. If you want to locate more elk, you need to be willing and prepared to get away from the roads.

This does not imply that you should be deceptive. I believe that honesty is by far the best policy, but a reasonable amount of tact and common sense is required if you want to learn something from this individual. One good source for these types of contacts is the local diner or coffee shop. Here most folks are a bit more relaxed and willing to share. They also feel secure on their own turf. Focus on that word, share. Any such discussion should be a two-way street. Perhaps you have some information of value for your contact. At least offer to buy the meal or coffee. Never take and run. Show genuine interest in what the other person has to say. One of the best icebreakers is to start off with common ground. Maybe you know someone in

town. Feel free to share a "war story" of yours about this common acquaintance. Chances are that if you are in elk country, your contact already has something in common with you—elk hunting! Finally, never dive directly into the part of the conversation about where to hunt. This means that you should treat him or her with the same respect that you would want to be treated.

Let me briefly touch on statistics. As we all know, anyone can make a set of statistics "talk" and make a convincing argument. The key to reliable statistics is the validity of the research that went into producing the data. The Division of Wildlife is not going to like this next remark, and someone there is sure to read this and I'll likely catch you know what for it, but sources within the division have been overheard (firsthand) to say that some herd stats published for public consumption are at times the figment of a game management officer's imagination, calculated to present a predetermined political objective for the individual or area. With that said, these stats are a fair source of information, but should be verified with a bit of personal detective work by interviewing locals.

Step #3: It's Time To Get Out the Topo Maps

Topographical maps come in a variety of forms and scales. Ultimately, you want to use a map with a good picture, including significant detail of the area you plan to hunt. There are a number of good topo map books on the market, like *Delorme's Colorado Atlas & Gazetteer* (scale 1:160,000 to 1:320,000) available for less than $20, that will allow you to get started with this process. The new editions also include GPS (global positioning system) data for those of you more technologically inclined. Once you have narrowed your hunt area to within say 16 square miles (42 sq km), head to your local supplier of USGS quad maps. Better yet, you can design, construct and purchase your own custom quad at my Web site (www.elkcamp.com).

These maps reflect a scale of 1:24,000 or 1:25,000 and show the greatest amount of detail. You can also obtain larger scale maps from the U.S. Forest Service or the Bureau of Land Management for a small fee. These maps generally fit in the former category of those maps good to start with and get a general feel for the lay of the land.

For those unfamiliar with map reading and the use of a good compass, there are numerous books at your local library or sporting goods supply store to help you acquire these skills, which are an absolute if you want to survive in elk country. If you prefer classroom-like instruction, many of the larger sporting goods chains and backpack supply outlets offer orienteering courses. These usually last a few hours and will equip you with enough basic orienteering skills to keep you out of all but extreme trouble.

Bulls are rarely found in the vicinity of roads. You'll need a good GPS and map to find your way into his lair.

Some guys were hunting national forest land in Colorado a few years back during the second combined rifle season. There were two or three other elk camps near theirs, all within a few hundred yards (m) of a state highway. In one of the other camps, a hunter had brought his wife along for company. She, however, preferred to remain in camp and read rather than traipse about all day like the rest of the hunters.

Each day this woman would place her lawn chair on the edge of their camp and read and watch smaller wildlife while cars and trucks passed by on the state road. Imagine the hunters' surprise one afternoon when they came back to camp and found this woman sitting in her chair with this big, you know what kind, grin on her face. She says, "Would you boys mind helping me for just a minute? I need some help getting that ole' elk up here to camp."

"What elk?" they asked.

"That 6 × 6 bull down yonder in the field by the road," she answered. "He just walked out of the timber over there by the creek and I just up and shot him with Jim's other rifle."

They never did ask her if she had her own license, and I surely do not advocate hunting without one. The woman and her husband were gone the next morning, so that may be the answer to that question. The point here is that from time to time elk can be found just about anywhere. Heck, I was darn near kamikazied by an elk herd one subzero winter morning before sunup, standing slap dab in the middle of I-25 just north of the U.S. Air Force Academy. Just goes to show you, but keep in mind, most elk are a bit more difficult to locate, so be prepared to work for it.

A well-placed camp allows the hunter to start hunting close to camp.

Step #4: Walk the Land

Many hunters new to an area show up on opening day never having laid eyes on the ground they intend to hunt. In many cases, especially with out-of-state hunters—who make up a significant number of those you meet—this unfamiliarity with the land places them at a distinct disadvantage. The more familiar you are with the terrain, the location of those hidden benches and holes (valley, for folks back East) that hold elk, the migration or travel routes, prevailing wind, sources of quality food and water, wallows, and so on, the higher the likelihood of putting meat in the freezer.

I'll really step out on a limb here and offer that without some amount of pre-season homework, your chances of bringing home a nice bull are about as likely as standing in camp, firing up in the air and hoping the bullet will bring down something. I realize that this is a fairly extreme comparison, but it should serve to get the point across: if you want to be successful at elk hunting, you have got to do your homework.

SIX REASONS ELK HUNTERS GO HOME EMPTY-HANDED

As elk hunters, we spend countless days and a fair portion of the family budget in pursuit of game, only to return home bone-tired, smelly, cold and, worst of all, empty-handed. So let's look at six reasons why elk hunters go home with empty coolers.

Reason #1: Lack of a Good Plan or Not Following the Plan

Do your homework! This means that if you want more success in your elk hunting endeavors, then you need to do a moderate amount of research into such things as: Where are the elk? How is your hunting party going to attack the problem of covering every inch (cm) of that area? And how are you going to manage the tags within your group? As you know, I love to tell stories that make a point. Here's one such story.

A few years ago my hunting partner and I took a whole bunch of guys with us elk hunting. As in most camps, old hunting friends chose to pair up and take to the woods in teams. I have no problem with such strategies.

I do it myself. One of the most rewarding aspects of elk hunting is the hours of camaraderie spent with good friends in pursuit of a wild and worthy adversary.

In this particular camp our number of bull tags and cow tags were about equal. So far so good, right? Well, yes and no. One would think that having a fair number of either type tag would be an overall smart plan. I agree it was. However, as our hunters partnered up each day to head out, guess how those tags were distributed? Let me tell you. About three-quarters of our hunters disregarded the type of tag their hunting partner had and we ended up with a bunch of cow tags going one way and a bunch of bull tags heading another. You can see this coming, can't you? Yep. The guys with bull tags ran into cows and the hunters with cow tags ran into bulls with neither having a legal opportunity to take a shot. On the next to the last morning of our hunt, two of our cow tag hunters walked up on two very nice shooter bulls. One was a large 6 × 6 and the other a very respectable 6 × 5.

Elk, particularly bulls, often find quality nourishment in small clearcuts or burns.

In late summer and early fall, elk are on a mission to acquire as much quality nutrition as they can. New-growth forage can be found in burns from as soon after a fire as three months, and as long as three years.

The 6 × 5 was broadside in the open at about 60 yards (55 m) and the 6 × 6 was around 200 yards (183 m) away. Although these two hunters came back to camp with a great story and life-long memory of the hunt, such stories are not quite as tasty as elk tenderloin, which might have been the outcome if at least one of the hunters had a bull tag.

If you want to defeat your adversary, if you want to survive, if you want to be successful, you have to have a plan to succeed and you must work that plan. Otherwise what may happen is chaos and you end up going home, often enough, empty-handed.

Reason #2: Poor Physical Condition

Elk hunting is hard work. Let me say this again. Elk hunting is hard work! Some of those factors that come into play in the course of a day of hunting such as weather or terrain are finite. By this I mean that there is not much that you can do to change these. The mountains are always going to be brutal on your lungs and your knees. The wind and the cold are forever going to be obstacles that we have to deal with. These are all a part of what we sign on for as elk hunters. There are factors that can become obstacles only if we allow them to become so.

Enjoying the adventure of elk hunting does not necessitate being in the physical shape of an Olympic athlete. But you do need to be in reasonably good shape. This means that whether you are thirty or fifty, you should be prepared to hike from 5 to as much as 15 miles (8 to 24 km) a day with all of your gear. It means that if you want to get into elk hunting, you have to be able and willing to do more than walk ¼ mile (0.4 km) from the truck and sit down and hope an elk stumbles by you.

If you want to be successful at elk hunting, you have to be able to go where the elk are, which means taking the time before your hunt to get into shape.

Reason # 3: Hunting Where There Are No Elk

You can have the best strategy and the hottest new gear, but if you're not hunting where the elk are, well . . . it sort of becomes a moot point, doesn't it? Elk, being creatures of habit, opportunity and need, are predictable as long as there are no external factors stirring up their day-to-day routine. By external factors I mean predators, particularly the two-legged gun-toting variety. Similar to human infants whose daily schedule is overly simplistic—eat, sleep, poop—the routine of the elk is fairly straightforward as well, revolving around what and where they eat.

Throughout the long days of summer, elk are content to graze on the sweet green grasses found in abundance below timberline and on high ridges. But as the days become noticeably shorter and summer fades into fall, nighttime temperatures drop below freezing and nature begins to shut off the nutrients that had supplied the grasses in the high country throughout the summer. Quite quickly the elk begin to notice the difference in the quality of their food supply. What was sweet and yummy just a few weeks ago is now becoming far less attractive to the elk's palate, much like a bag of store-bought salad that has been opened and left in the refrigerator too long. Consequently, in early autumn the elk often move down the mountain to lower elevations where the graze has yet to be affected by the colder temperatures.

Such transitions are evident by the effect on agriculture at these lower elevations. Alfalfa fields are favorites for elk. Unlike other grasses, which die off rather quickly after the first frosts, alfalfa remains green for weeks and the elk know this. Once the elk locate a good patch of alfalfa, they have been known to travel miles (km) to get at it, feeding throughout the night and heading back up the mountain before daylight.

Another way to determine if the elk have moved down low is to check the status of ranchers' haystacks in the area. Haystacks can be a prime source of elk feed. Once hay is cut, baled and stacked, it doesn't take long for the outer layers of the bales to turn brown. Take a quick scouting trip around your hunting area to see if any of the haystacks have been worked over by elk. If the fresh greenish yellow hay beneath the outer layer is visible, it's a clue where the elk might be, or at least where they're feeding.

Elk often frequent sources of water like streams and springs, after feeding at night prior to heading back to their bedding areas for the day.

Once the frost line begins to move down the mountain, the lowlands' graze begins to lose its appeal and the elk usually move back up the mountain to feed, as the grasses up high have now cured and become attractive nourishment again.

In drought years, water sources can also be an excellent place to find elk. Find the water and you will find the elk. If the high country has had plenty of rain or the snow pack from the previous winter has left streams with water in them, this tactic doesn't work as well.

After feeding throughout the night, elk begin making their way back up the mountain to their bedding areas in the timber before sunrise. A smart hunter will arrive at elk camp three to four days ahead of the season and spend time glassing the area in the early morning and late evening hours to locate the elks' travel routes between their feeding and bedding areas.

Finally, give the elk a break on the day before the season opens. This is one mistake I see all too

Bulls are large-bodied animals. A quartering-away shot offers the prepared hunter a excellent opportunity to harvest a bull.

often. Hunters with a year's worth of pent-up frustration get to elk camp on Friday before the season opener on Saturday and cannot wait to get out in the woods and find some elk. Do you ever wonder why the elk are all over the place before the season and somehow seem to disappear on opening day? Ever think it might have something to do with a few hundred hunters traipsing all over the same hunting area on Friday afternoon between 2 p.m. and dark?

If your plan to bushwhack the elk on the way back from their feeding area fails to produce, then the real tough hunt begins. The elk have made it back into their bedding areas in the timber, and if you hope to have a crack at one, you're going to have to go in and get him. In this hunter's opinion, this is the toughest hunting there is, but if you want to hunt where the elk are, during late morning and midday it's the black timber.

Reason # 4: Hunting Short Days and Sleeping Long Nights

Successful elk hunters are committed elk hunters. They are willing to endure hardships not typically encountered hunting other North American game. Rising hours before dawn in frigid tents, often without any form of heat, these hunters must begin the day by kicking off the layer of ice that formed overnight from the condensation of their breath on top of their sleeping bags.

Some of the smart ones will have placed their hunting clothes between their sleeping bag and their cot or ground pad, further insulating their bedding from the cold and using their body heat to warm the clothing throughout the long fall night. Others willingly endure jumping into half-frozen pants and shirts. Either way, they are up with a cup of coffee and heading out for elk country long before the eastern sky has thought about becoming light. Their daypack is filled with everything that they will require to remain in the field until the last ray of twilight has faded in the west. The thought of coming back to camp for an afternoon siesta has never entered their thinking, for these are true hunters. They know that bringing a great bull elk to ground is no simple task.

They have planned to stay out every day for as long as it takes. They have waited for these moments all year, and some may have waited an entire lifetime. These are the men and women I admire. These are hunters who rarely come home empty-handed.

Reason # 5: Hunting the Easy Ground

Can you hunt elk sitting in a lawn chair on an open hillside 500 feet (152 m) from a blacktop road with a cooler full of your favorite refreshment nearby? Absolutely, yes you can. Can you see or even hope to kill elk from such a stand? Maybe. Will you? Hmmmm. My educated guess? More than likely, not. While I may have gone a bit overboard with the lawn chair and cooler reference, every year we see hundreds upon hundreds of hunters who want an easy hunt. They cruise Forest Service roads for hours until they spy a particular spot that to them "looks like an elk spot." What does an elk spot look like? How big is it? What color is it? Does it smell like elk? What exactly makes one place look like elk will appear in it more than another? If someone knows, please tell me! The only for sure elk spot I know of is one that has an elk standing right in the middle of it.

High points offer the hunter an excellent observation position from which to glass for elk.

Anyhow, once they have found their elk spot, they pull the truck and camper out of the center of the road, leaving just enough of the back end sticking out as to give the next guy coming around the curve a near heart attack. Next this fellow hauls out his trusty rifle, struggles into his one-size-too-small blaze orange vest, and walks 100 yards (91 m) down the hill, lights up a cigarette and perches himself on a rock for the remainder of the day. This is what some of us call "staking out" the easy ground. Notice that I did not say hunting.

Remember, elk are herd animals and as such the entire elk population of a given area may pass within a few hundred yards (m) of the sedentary hunter, completely unnoticed. This hunter is far less likely to encounter elk than the hunter who spends the day working hard and wisely covering as much territory as possible.

Reason # 6: Hunting from ATVs

Those of you who have spent any measurable amount of time elk hunting public land knew this one was coming. First, let me say for the record, that just like

pickup trucks and campers and such, ATVs or OHVs or whatever you choose to call them can play a useful role in the overall elk hunting experience. When there are hundreds of pounds (kgs) of elk on the ground and miles (km) between the hunter and camp, these vehicles—when used appropriately and in accordance with the laws and regulations established for the area that is being hunted—can be a huge benefit.

Unfortunately each year more and more would-be hunters are taking to the field and literally hunting from their ATVs, even though this act is illegal in many states.

If you own an ATV and want to take it with you elk hunting, by all means do so. It is your right. Just remember to respect the rights of your fellow hunters and use your vehicle responsibly and within the law.

I have been elk hunting the high country for over eighteen years and I have never seen, met or heard of anyone who has taken an elk while hunting from any type of motor vehicle. If you need to ride your truck or ATV from camp up a legally marked road to some point of advantage, go for it. Then park it and put your hunt plan into action.

ATV EXTREMES

Two years ago I was hunting with a group of friends in south central Colorado. It was mid-morning on the third day of our hunt. I was on a stand overlooking a large meadow in what I considered to be a reasonably remote location a mile (1.6 km) or so from the end of the nearest jeep trail and many miles (km) from a designated road. The only trails of any kind in sight were game trails.

I had been sitting on this particular stand about an hour when I picked up the sound of ATVs approaching from somewhere down the ridge behind me. Since they sounded like they were coming toward me, I looked at my watch to see how long it would take them to get to my position. Almost 10 minutes later two guys astride their ATVs came riding down the game trail—in formation—a mere 20 yards (18 m) behind me, shouting to one another at the tops of their lungs so as to be heard over the cacophony of their machines.

I could hear that racket for 10 full minutes, and I bet every elk in the area could hear it as well, and had left for places unknown far ahead of these fellows. To add insult to injury, they stopped about 50 yards (46 m) from my 7 o'clock position and, with engines running, took a smoke break. I was in clear view, all decked out in blaze orange. I know they saw me, because one of them pointed directly at me.

It wasn't until two of my hunting partners walked up the same game trail and joined me, and disgusted by what these guys had just done, the three of us began to walk in their direction that they came to their senses and left.

What a morning! My hunting partners said they were going to try another area on the far side of the mountain and I couldn't blame them. We parted ways and I remained on my stand for a while, trying to come up with a new plan.

My hunting buddies had been gone for about 15 minutes when I heard what I initially thought was another ATV coming up the trail from the opposite direction, only this one seemed a bit more quiet than the last two. As I continued to look in that direction, you can image my shock when lo and behold coming up this rocky game trail that is only about 20 inches (51 cm) wide are two hunters in blaze orange hats in a front-wheel-drive blue minivan!

Twice in one day? I decided to go hunt another mountain.

When you have any species of game on the ground, an ATV can make hauling the meat back to camp a lot easier.

GLASSING AND OPTICS

For scouting, nothing beats a good spotting scope and tripod. Binoculars are excellent for glassing during the hunt, but when glassing for prolonged periods, a spotting scope on a tripod significantly reduces your physical effort, and the higher levels of magnification often help you to spot and classify that far-off bull that might not be as visible with binoculars.

Here are some factors to consider when purchasing a spotting scope: How will you be using the scope? Will you be glassing slopes from your vehicle on a road, or will you be packing the scope into the backcountry? If so, how much weight can you afford to add to your pack? How much do you have in your budget?

More than once I have said, "Don't go cheap on optics. Buy the best optics that you can afford." More expensive scopes usually offer a higher-quality and often a lighter-weight optical product for a given magnification capacity. Unless you have an unlimited budget, however, there will come a point where you have to ask yourself what is the best you can buy without breaking the bank and incurring the wrath of your family. Over the years I have tried optics—binoculars and spotting scopes—from one end of the spectrum to the other and have concluded that I do not have to spend the kids' college education money to acquire good optics.

Spot-and-stalk elk hunting means long hours glassing for elk.

Quality binoculars make all the difference!

Alpen Optics of Rancho Cucamonga, California, a relatively new player on the sports optics scene (1997), produces first-class optics at a very affordable price. Key criteria that I look for when purchasing optics are:
- clarity at all light levels with an exit pupil of 4–5 mm
- weatherproof
- lightweight (24–28 ounce/680–794 g for binoculars and 25–30 ounce/709–850 g for spotting scopes)
- shock-resistant
- fully multi-coated lenses to prevent the glass surfaces from reflecting or losing light
- a longer eye relief because I wear glasses

Good binoculars are one help to hunters trying to locate elk in dense stands of timber.

My optics setup includes a first-rate pair of Alpen Rainier 10 × 42 binoculars and a spotting scope, a high-power variable magnification scope for glassing very long distances from roads. My scope is an Alpen Model 788 20-60 × 80 with a 45-degree eyepiece.

As you can see, I have become a one-manufacturer kind of guy. The reason? When I find a great product supported by a team of professionals at an affordable price, I go for it.

If a spotting scope is not in the budget this year, then consider upgrading your binoculars. For years I have hunted day in and day out with 10 × 42 roof prism binoculars. My Alpen Rainier binoculars are the perfect all-around elk hunting binocular. The 42mm objective

lens significantly increases the low light capability during the prime elk hunting times of early morning and evening.

It's important to minimize the amount of pressure you put on the elk during your scouting. Using quality optics allows you to cover more territory in less time without having to pressure the game.

Also, keep to higher ground when at all possible. Spend more time glassing from prominent lookouts and less time busting brush. Save this for the actual hunt. If you are able to get a fix on these travel routes, it's time to get your map out and plan your ambush, taking into account terrain and the prevailing wind.

Chapter 2

LEARNING ABOUT ELK BEHAVIOR

Hunting elk is very different from hunting whitetails. Other than having four legs and antlers, the differences really outnumber the similarities.

I have hunted elk for almost twenty years and not a year goes by that I do not run into hunters in the field who, when queried, show a clear lack of knowledge about elk behavior. If we look at the overall harvest statistics, we find that the average elk hunter is successful once in every eight years.

Granted, there are many hunters whose success rate is far in excess of this ratio, but on the other hand there are many, many elk hunters who go home with empty coolers year after year because they just will not take the time to gain even a basic understanding of elk and how they use elk country. They assume that either it must be similar to deer hunting or that they can just figure it out on the fly.

Whitetail habitat typically ranges from lowland farm country and woodlots to open prairie. Hardwoods like oak, hickory and maple are common browse for deer. With few exceptions, whitetails are found at elevations from sea level to about 4,000 feet (1,219 m). Elk, on the other hand, can be found in open pasture at 5,000 feet (1,524 m), but primarily inhabit much higher and more rugged mountain terrain, covered in a variety of pines and firs as well as aspen, ranging from 8,000 feet (2,438 m) to well above timberline and altitudes of 12,000 (3,657 m) and greater.

Jay's Tip

The key is to cover as much ground as possible.

Whitetails are primarily browsers, meaning they prefer to eat from the tree or brush as opposed to the ground. Elk, like cattle, prefer to graze on grass, succulents and other feed found on or very near the ground. Granted, either will shift their feeding grounds depending on their needs and what is available, but their preferences remain the same.

Where deer are far more solitary animals traveling mostly as singles or in smaller groups, elk are herd animals that live and travel in groups ranging from a few animals to hundreds. This is a plains game behavior from the times when elk inhabited flatter and more open terrain.

One summer a few years ago, I was invited on a summer pack trip in the Flat Tops Wilderness Area of Colorado. I decided to combine this opportunity with a little scouting. It was early July, so the bulls and cows were mostly split up at this time. The ride in took maybe three hours, but in the course of one of those hours on horseback, we saw and filmed approximately 600 to 700 head of elk, all traveling in large groups of 50 to 300. This is not to say that you can expect to see groups of this size regularly. It is to reinforce my point that elk travel primarily in groups.

The longest tine on an elk's rack is usually the fourth point; sometimes called the sword point or dagger point. By visually locating this point and counting the points to the rear, you can quickly determine the total number of points. The bull shown here is a 6x6.

The norm for elk is to travel in groups.

I wish I could tell you how many times I've heard some hunter say, "There aren't any elk around here." Well, maybe there are and maybe there aren't. Any given area may hold a quantity of elk, but if you don't know how to maximize your chances of locating these elk, you are likely to respond similarly. So how can you maximize this opportunity"?

Here's an example.

You are hunting an area that is approximately 2 miles square (5 sq km) and is known to hold 100 animals. Granted, this is a rather small area but for purposes of this example, just bear with me.

Conventional deer hunting strategy says to look for game trails, signs or areas that would provide a source of food or water, and set up a stand. Your stand might be a tree stand, a ground blind or just hiding behind a tree. Either way, you have done your homework and now you have staked out a point of ambush, right? Well maybe, but probably not.

Why? As I mentioned earlier, deer travel in singles and small groups, so the probability of one of those 100 deer inhabiting the 2-square-mile (5 sq km) area walking somewhere close to your stand are fairly good, but let's consider the travel patterns of elk.

Remember, elk travel in herds. Here I will be conservative and assume that the same 100 animals (elk) are moving about in the same 2-square-mile (5 sq km) area. If the same hunter sets up in the same stationary blind, what do you think his or her chances are of seeing these elk that may all be traveling together or in a few family groups? Let's say that the stand is over a wallow on the edge of a small meadow that is 500 yards (457 m) long and 500 yards (457 m) wide, which is fairly large as some go.

All it takes is for the elk herd to pass you in the dark timber by a few yards (m). Believe me, you would be surprised how quiet a herd of elk can be, tiptoeing through the woods and causing you to miss the entire event. If you are honest, you'll admit that a hunter's chances of locating the elk from a stationary stand are significantly less than the chances would have been for locating deer.

FIND THE FOOD, FIND THE ELK

Experienced elk hunters, terrestrial biologists, DNR officials, and this writer agree, an elk's number one priority is locating and consuming food of the highest nutritional value available. Ninety percent of an elk's day is spent feeding and resting. While other needs may rank high, absolutely nothing supersedes an elk's dietary requirements. Not security and not breeding—survival is about food. Without the essential nutrition that elk acquire by feeding, all else is pretty much a moot point. If you are serious about elk hunting, learn about their feeding habits.

When I began researching the subject matter that would eventually become the "meat and potatoes" of this book, I searched out the critical information that seemed missing or only minimally addressed in other hunting literature. To my surprise, at the top of the list were elk feeding habits. I thought, how could such an essential topic manage to acquire so little attention? Like humans and all other creatures, elk need food to exist. Cell generation and repair, respiration, circulation, propagation, gestation, fight or flight—each aspect of existence requires fuel to function. Nutrition is the key ingredient to survival.

Therefore, this discussion will focus on elk feeding habits, including the differences between the feeding habits of bull and cow elk. Learning the specifics of how and why elk feed as they do leads to a better understanding of the elk in general, which helps us better predict where elk will be at a given time.

New-growth forest is like an energy bar to elk. It provides large quantities of nutrients essential to preparing for survival of the coming winter.

Thick cover along creek bottoms offer elk a secure access to water sources.

When planning a hunt, factor into the plan two established aspects of elk behavior. First, elk are exceedingly opportunistic—they are adaptable and will take advantage of favorable situations. It is this opportunism that has caused elk to become such a migratory creature, seizing upon a variety of food sources. How does this play out for the hunter?

In the fall, when the high-nutrition forage required to make it through the rut and the following winter months becomes more and more scarce, elk are motivated to continually travel to new growth food sources as they become available. They exploit each new source until the food is depleted or other factors, such as extreme weather or predators, force them to move on. Sources of new growth forage change as the season progresses from late August into the early winter months. In late August and early September, new growth can still be found throughout most elk summer range in open grasslands, moist secluded forests, near valley floor seeps and along water sources near the heads of drainages.

This broad dispersal of food sources with high nutritional value helps explain why elk may be in a particular drainage today and in another drainage tomorrow.

A fall snow can stimulate elk movement. The smart hunter remains afield waiting for the elk to move after the storm.

Once the frosts of mid- to late September begin to affect the quality of food in a particular area, the elk continually move on in search of quality forage.

When adverse weather—either too warm or too cold—moves into the area, elk herds usually break into smaller groups and seek the late-season new growth and security found on the forest floor in heavily timbered tracts. The forest floor also offers a protective thermal barrier from cold weather. This shift from open-area grazing to forests is usually abrupt, because it typically coincides with the beginning of hunting season. While hunting pressure is a factor in the transition, research indicates that this movement is related more to the availability of forage with high nutritional value and changes in temperature.

As freezing nights take their toll on grassland food sources, elk transition from graze to browse and their use of forested areas increase. Along with the onset of hunting seasons is the rut, which also affects the elk foraging patterns. Bulls and cows alike now make reproduction a priority for a short period of time.

Young bulls sparring.

When a bull bugles, he secretes a fluid from his pre-orbital gland located just forward of each eye. This fluid is then often transferred to trees in the area as a form of advertisement to cows.

It is during the rut that bulls may burn off as much as 30 percent of their accumulated body fat herding and breeding, leaving them in a severely energy-depleted state going into winter.

Following the rut, with the possible exception of a few younger bulls, the cows and bulls separate. Studies suggest that it is the bulls that choose to leave the cows. Factors that influence this decision are that bulls, having expended large amounts of energy, must make the most of the time remaining to build fat stores before the deep snows of winter arrive. To avoid competing for essential forage with the cows, whose reproductive priorities are to optimize security for calves over quality forage, the bulls depart the herd for areas where competition is less.

Bulls keep close watch on cows, until the breeding time is right.

By the time the rut begins, antler velvet will be gone, splitting in long pieces and shed in a day or two. The antlers are then strong enough for bush thrashing and dominance battles.

After the rigors of the rut, bulls become solitary, as they struggle to regain fat reserves before winter.

Larger, more mature herd bulls that have expended more of their energy and fat reserves usually seek the best opportunities they can find for food, as well as refuge from hunters, in secluded forested tracts at the highest elevations. Another factor for this dispersal of cows and bulls is predation.

As the snow becomes deeper in the high country, an elk's ability to flee is impaired and antlered bulls in a herd of cows easily stand out to predators; thus remaining with the herd increases their risk of becoming a target, especially older bulls. Separating from the cows and seeking out more secluded feeding and bedding areas make bulls more secure.

The second aspect of elk behavior to consider when planning a hunt concerns what Jack Ward Thomas and Dale E. Toweill in their 1982 book *Elk of North*

America: Ecology and Management refer to as the Law of Least Effort. This means that, for a maximum benefit, the resources that elk require must be obtained with a minimum of effort. This rule is predominant in elk behavior and is supported by the amount of time elk invest in eating and resting, as discussed earlier. The balance of their day, 10 percent or less, is spent standing and walking around, usually near their bedding areas, the objective being to store up as much energy and fat as possible, while burning minimal calories.

Elk behavior in winter, such as walking single file in deep snow, feeding in softer, shallow snow or migrating to lower areas where they do not have to work as hard to feed is evidence of this.

I admit that for years I failed to give much attention to the differences in the feeding patterns of cow elk and those of bulls. In recent years, however, with the increased hunting pressure on public lands, finding the elk has become the number one challenge. Like most hunters, we applied what might be called a brute-force strategy when the elk appeared to become scarce; we hunted harder and longer. Unfortunately, this plan failed to produce the expected result. It was this failed strategy that I have witnessed or learned from year after year in camp after camp that forced me to examine how most elk hunters hunt and what can be done to help them become more successful.

As a professional hunting consultant, writer and conference speaker on elk hunting, I have access to some of the best minds in the industry, from which I gather essential information on elk, elk hunting and elk country. From guides and outfitters, to professional hunters, elk biologists, game managers, wildlife officers and others, the answer to my search for a better strategy was the same: If you want to get to the elk, you have to hunt smarter! If you want to become more successful elk hunters in an ever-increasing environment of high-pressured elk, you have to learn more about the elk themselves.

Solitary bulls seek out secluded and often difficult-to-access hideaways after the rut. Post-rut hunters seeking a trophy will have to hunt in some of the most challenging terrain.

Bulls versus Cows

So how is a cow's feeding behavior different from that of a bull? Due the cow's role in reproduction, cow elk are better able to acquire and store fat and nutrients from the forage they feed on during summer and fall.

As a result of this ability, the cow is not as dependent on high-quality feed and thus can ingest more fibrous material than a bull during long winter months, and is not as pressured to continually seek new food sources.

Bulls, on the other hand, especially the older bulls sought by hunters, must pack away all the high-quality nutrients they can find.

Jay's Tip

A cow's extra reserves also mean she will not have to feed as much or as often in winter. This allows cows to focus more on protecting their calves from predators. Large cow-calf herds that gather for mutual security throughout the winter demonstrate this.

The average bull consumes as much as 12 pounds (5.4 kg) of forage per day. If he hopes to survive the extreme winter temperatures of elk country, avoid predators and reproduce, he must focus his post-rut efforts on maximizing his intake while minimizing his exertion—again, the law of least effort. As a vital player in the future of the gene pool, he must not compete with the cows that are responsible for producing and protecting the next generation.

Lead cow standing guard.

Due to his larger body size and antlers, the bull can afford to trade off security for forage. Soon after the rut ends, bulls begin to drift away from the cow-calf herd in search of nutrient-rich food. If the forage is plentiful, less mature bulls may re-form small bachelor groups, as they did in the summer. Older, larger bulls, on the other hand, become quite solitary and reclusive.

Bulls, again because of their larger body size and ability to absorb more heat, must disperse significantly more retained heat than cows. This requirement leads bulls to seek cooler areas in which to feed and rest, such as dark timber, blowdowns and shady north-facing slopes on warmer days or days of bright sun.

Typically, larger bulls are the last to evacuate the cooler high country when winter snows begin to accumulate. I have often been asked, "How much snow does it take to move elk out of the high country?" My hip-pocket response is that when the snow depth reaches an elk's belly, it starts looking for an easier place to find lunch. For cow elk this may be 14 to 18 inches (36 to 46 cm), while for bulls it may take as much as 24 inches (61 cm) of snow to move them to another area.

Jay's Tip

Keep in mind that there are no hard and fast numbers on the factors that may affect when elk begin to move down the mountain in search of an easier-to-obtain meal. Be flexible and be aware of changing conditions.

Hunting Burns

When it comes to the types of habitat in which we as hunters can expect to locate elk, one that seems to cause a fair amount of discussion is that of small burns—that is, areas that have been burned over in a past forest fire. Burns can play a vital role in the ecosystem for elk, though perhaps not as vital for cows as for bulls. Nutrient-rich forage in burn areas may begin to reappear within just a few months of a fire.

The tender new shoots tend to attract elk for as long as three years after a fire. Small burns offer bulls a source of quality nutrients for building fat reserves, and minerals for antler development during the summer. In fall, these same areas provide excellent forage that helps bulls survive the winter. Cow elk that use open-area herding as a form of protection from predators do not frequent small burns as much as bulls.

Look for bulls in small burns.

The bulk of an elk's day is spent feeding and bedding—again, roughly 90 percent— with prime daytime feeding in the first few hours after sunrise and the last few hours before sunset. Bedding takes up the majority of the time in between. This schedule changes dramatically, however, during the rut. Focused on reproducing, both cows and bulls now spend many of their bedding hours traveling or standing.

Feeding continues to take up the lion's share of a day, but rutting and rut-related activity seems to override the need for sleep, especially for bulls. In the normal course of a 24-hour period, elk feed and bed both day and night. During summer months the feeding patterns of elk remain about the same with regard to daytime or nighttime feeding. However, the amount of time that they spend bedding at night nearly doubles from 20 to 40 percent in winter, as the elk attempt to optimize the use of every available calorie. Again, the law of least effort.

Feeding in groups maximizes the chance of sensing danger nearby.

BUGLING, A HIGH COUNTRY SYMPHONY

Not too long ago I was bowhunting a steep alder-covered slope in northern Idaho when, out of nowhere and without the least bit of warning, my hunting partner and I were enveloped by a raspy, guttural roaring from somewhere close by. As the sheer volume of sound echoed around me, the hairs on the back of my neck stood straight up and I instinctively dropped to one knee in some sort of prehistoric hunter's defensive posture, wondering what was about to run over me. In mere seconds my body was flooded with about a gallon and a half of adrenaline and my fight-or-flight mechanism came to full alert.

In that part of the state the cover is so dense that during five days of hunting, I had four similar up-close and personal encounters with bulls screaming their heads off at me, yet I only saw one.

The typical mature elk bugle frequently consists of three parts. The bugle begins with a low-frequency raspy sound emanating from deep in the bull's gut, then gradually rises to a high-pitched scream that can carry quickly across as many as three octaves, often holding the highest note before promptly falling off to another low-frequency series of grunts or chuckles.

Bugling bull.

A bull's "advertisement" bugle can go on a long time.

During the rut, a bull's bugle is his way of saying "Pick me" to a cow in estrus.

A quick review of Physics 101 tells us that sound propagation is not as much a function of volume as it is of frequency. While volume (energy output) is a factor, it is the frequency of the sound that determines how far and through how much cover the sound can travel without distortion. High-frequency sounds, such as those in the second part of an elk bugle or scream, travel relatively short distances, even though they are powered by a greater volume of air. Lower frequency sounds like those in the early stages of a bugle or the ending chuckle carry for longer distances.

This physics is also evidenced by the U.S. Navy's use of ELF, or Extra Low Frequency sound, for communicating with its submarines that may be submerged and on patrol thousands of miles (km) away from the source.

Bugling is first and foremost a means of advertisement to cows and bulls alike. In a way, the bull is saying to every cow around, "Pick me. I am the guy that you are looking for." It is not a challenge to fight other bulls in the valley, as many elk hunters believe. According to renowned elk researcher Valerius Geist, bulls bugle in an attempt to out-advertise one another.

It is the method bulls use to attract cows for reproduction and, when necessary, to announce to any interloper bulls nosing around the periphery of the herd that they claim the cows in their harem.

Bulls also bugle during the mating ritual. Since it is the cow that determines with which bull and when she will mate, bulls that make unwanted sexual advances to a cow that is not ready are often met with. . . well, rejection. The cow just walks off in a submissive posture.

After such rejection, the bull may emit a shortened version of his bugle, perhaps as some vocal signal of frustration. On the flip side, when bulls successfully mount a cow that is ready to mate, the act is violently quick and typically ends with the bull jumping clear off the ground followed by a bugle. Go figure.

URINE SPRAYING

If much of the behavior elk exhibit during the rut is about self-promotion, then I would be remiss if I failed to talk about urine spraying. That's right, bull elk peeing all over themselves. No one ever said bull elk were much into personal hygiene and this definitely confirms it. In reality, urine spraying during the rutting ritual is another way that bulls advertise themselves.

Late one September, my wife, Rae Ann, and I were attending Elk Fest in Estes Park, Colorado. Our workday had come to an end around 5 p.m., so we decided to take a tour around town to try to get some pictures of any of the hundreds of elk that frequently wander through town during that time of the year. I know, this doesn't sound like much of a hunting story and it isn't; it's an elk behavior story and you observe elk behavior wherever the elk happen to be. This particular story took place on the Estes Park city golf course.

When we arrived at the golf course, we saw about 200 elk herded up into roughly four small groups grazing on some really nice Bermuda grass on one of the course's fairways. Each group was under the watchful eye of a dominant or herd bull, with two to four satellite bulls drifting around the edge of each group, presumably looking for an opportunity to sneak in and breed one of the cows.

The herd bulls were doing a first-rate job, running back and forth from one end of their respective harem to another chasing off raghorn after raghorn, all the while bugling at the top of their lungs to let the cows know who was in charge. This was clearly a form of advertisement, as we saw no challenges to these brutes during our two hours of observation. While watching one particular herd, I did notice a nice 5 × 5 satellite bull that was starting to behave more aggressively. In one instance this particular bull decided that he had enough of these two-legged creatures (people) encroaching on what he must have considered his territory, so he chased three of them over a fence.

Hopeful satellite bulls are often found along the periphery of the herd during the rut.

For bulls, the rut is about convincing cows to choose him as a breeding partner—in the deep cover or on the golf course!

It was pretty comical: one minute these tourists are snapping away with their digital cameras without a care in the world, even though some are within 20 yards (18 m) of a pretty worked-up bull and then all I could see were flip-flops and backsides flying over the fence. I thought I was going to split something, I laughed so hard.

After running off the two-legged competition, this bull must have been thinking pretty highly of himself as he began to spray. Spraying can take a number of forms, from a light mist to a semi-directed stream, to a very heavy conical spray. The urine in most cases is directed at nearly right angles to the erected penis.

Lowering his head almost to the ground, the bull began in the semi-directed stream mode by spraying his face briefly, then moving rearward to spray the heavy mane under his neck. He worked this area over for a good minute. All the while, the bull is palpitating. Palpitation is a rhythmic throbbing of the light-colored area behind the

penis and can be easily seen as it bobs during the spraying.

Occasionally this particular bull would seemingly lose control of his aim, as the urine stream would fire off to the left or right, pretty much hosing down anything within 4 or 5 feet (1.2 or 1.5 m). Fortunately, all the tourists in colorful shorts and flip-flops were well out of range by now. Once the bull had exhausted what I thought must have been a gallon (3.8 l) or more, the spraying ceased and the bull knelt down and began to rub and roll around in the overspray that had fallen on the ground—presumably to make sure that nothing went to waste.

Actually, the urine-soaked ground had muddied up pretty good and made for a fine, yet small, wallow. Often bulls follow up this behavior by rubbing their recently soaked neck mane and the preorbital glands below their eyes on a nearby tree, leaving some of the urine-soaked mud that they picked up in the wallow as another form of territorial advertisement.

HERDING AND HAREM DEFENSE

The rut is a time of competition, collection, advertisement and dominance. Cows seek out dominant bulls as a way of narrowing the field and assuring themselves that they have access to the best genetics for reproduction. Bulls are continually advertising to attract cows, conditioning the cows to remain nearby and, when necessary, herding the cows to keep them from straying.

I recently observed two groups of cows, each accompanied by a herd bull. Both groups were feeding on opposite sides of a small creek. If I had to estimate, I would guess that the groups were about 200 yards (183 m) apart, yet the creek seemed to act as a physical barrier keeping the groups from mingling.

For the better part of an hour the cows were content to remain in their respective groups. All the while each bull was on full-time guard duty, bugling and running from one end of his harem to another consoling his cows, keeping them nearby and running off the younger satellite bulls that would from time to time make a run at one of the females. The bulls appeared to be equally matched in the five-year age range, one a nice 6 × 6 and the other a 6 × 7. Either of these bulls would have made a grand addition to any elk hunter's wall. Unfortunately for me, hunting season was already complete, and I was confined to the sidelines with only a camera.

Antlers laid back is a herding posture—very effective with the harem cows.

Bulls sometimes need to encourage harem cows back to the herd, gently pushing them in the right direction.

As I observed the two groups I wondered what would happen if a few of these cows decided to cross the creek to the other bull. It was not long before I got my answer when a single cow dropped down into the creek and made her way over to the herd on the opposite side. I watched the two bulls to see how they would react.

While the gaining bull (bull #1) didn't seem to take much notice, the losing bull (bull #2) that had been at the far end of the herd was getting pretty worked up. Regrettably for him there were two raghorns flirting around his end of the herd and he couldn't risk responding to the cow's departure with anything other than a parting "please come back sweetheart" bugle.

Always vigilant, bulls stand watch over their harem, guarding against a surprise predator approach.

When cows come into estrus, they may be receptive to breeding for only a matter of hours.

I continued to watch bull #1 on the opposite bank to see if there would be any sign of victory when a second collared cow and her yearling calf started to make their way down into the creek about 5 minutes after the first. As she climbed the opposite bank, I guess her former boyfriend, bull #2, noticed her and this was about all he could take.

Even though he appeared to be outweighed by the darker bull on the opposite side of the creek by at least 100 pounds (45 kg), bull #2 let out a husky roar and charged down the meadow about 75 yards (69 m) and across the creek. I said to myself, "This is going to be good," as I waited for the battle to begin.

Bull #2 ran directly into the center of the cows on the opposite bank, stretched his neck and began to bugle and palpitate. Two things happened. The few cows that had scattered when he ran into the harem began to settle down and return to the group, and the larger, darker bull #1 immediately trotted about 300 yards (274 m) away in complete submission.

Clearly bull #2, even with lesser body size, was able to make up the difference using a more assertive dominance display. Within 10 minutes, with bull #1 now grazing farther down the meadow, alone in defeat, the rest of bull #2's harem moved across the stream to join the newly acquired harem and form a single group of about 50 cows.

Whenever one of the cows would begin to drift away, the new herd bull would lower his head below his shoulders, toss his antlers rearward along his back and move toward the offending cow at an angle with his eyes averted, often making a few grunts to console and encourage the cow to return to the herd.

If the wayward cow failed to comply with this form of gentle persuasion, the bull would bring his antlers forward and make mock charges at the cow as a further enticement to get back in line. On a few occasions, I have actually witnessed bulls rush the cow and even horn them if their response was not what the bull wanted. Many times once the cow started to move back toward the herd, the bull would turn away from the cow and bugle. Since cows are really running the show, this bugle is more symbolic of the bull recognizing and acknowledging the cow's decision to submit and return to the herd.

Unlike herding behavior, a bull intent on mating with a particular cow usually approaches the cow from a more head-on direction with his antlers fully erect. This communicates to the cow that his intent is other than merely herding. A cow that shows interest will allow the bull to move around behind her, where he begins licking her to determine if she has come into season yet. If the cow is not yet ready or decides that this bull is not the guy she wants to dance with after all, she usually moves away and displays a sign of submission. If she determines that the bull is "the guy," she assumes a rear-leg spread, haunch-low posture. Many times you can actually see the cow's rear legs quiver as she prepares for the bull.

This brief discussion is offered to demonstrate that while herding prior to mating is essential, the bull's attention is predominantly focused on acquiring and holding cows. Hunters who are aware of this period of diverted attention should use this to their advantage by creating a plan to close for the shot, especially if bowhunting. It is critical to keep in mind, however, that while the bull's attention may be diverted, he is surrounded by perhaps dozens of sets of eyes (cows) that are continually looking for other prospective mates, and predators as well.

Your challenge is to close to within effective shooting range without alerting the cows. Here you have to pay attention to the wind. As cows are continually moving about the periphery of the herd, you can try using your cow call to make soft comforting mews to cover unexpected footfalls as you move in. If you pay close attention to the wind and use cover, however, you would be better to move in with no sound at all, as any sound can attract attention. The less attention you draw to yourself, the better off you will be. Keep in mind that when stalking bulls that are herding cows, your real challenge is to beat the cows' defense mechanism.

If you want to score on a large herd bull, you will have to first avoid detection from a dozen or more sets of eyes—the cows.

TRAVEL PATTERNS

Remember, elk spend roughly 90 percent of their time—the exception being the rut—eating and resting. So how do they spend the remaining hours of any 24-hour period? The areas in which elk feed throughout early to mid-fall (hunting season) and the habitat in which they rest during the day to digest can be separated by significant distances, often miles (km). Taking the time to study and understand how elk transition from one area to the other, and the factors that may affect why elk use these specific routes, significantly increases your chance at scoring on a high-beamed bull or a fat cow, compared with randomly traversing elk country, taking your rifle or bow for an extended walk.

Keep in mind our previous discussion on the Law of Least Effort, as elk use the same established trails year after year.

Old travel routes usually found on timbered north- or east-facing slopes not only provide security but also make for easier travel. For travel between drainages, elk like to use saddles, often approaching them not straight on, which requires a lot more effort, but by using existing trails that run nearly parallel but just below the ridgetop so as not to highlight themselves.

If the saddle is open or exposed, elk may move left or right for cover soon after crossing the ridge. If there is open territory on the far side of the saddle with little cover, elk may pause or slow for a minute to make sure that the coast is clear before entering a meadow. If cover is available within the saddle itself, elk almost always remain in the cover. In either case, placing a stand or setting up just over the saddle may give you an opportunity for a shot at a stationary or slow-moving elk.

Elk walking single file in deep winter snow is a good example of The Law of Least Effort.

Whenever possible, elk travel in cover.

Elk have been known to use old stock trails in areas that are subject to summer grazing by cattle once the cattle have been moved out of the area to lower pasture. If you happen to come across a well-used stock trail, look closely for signs of elk usage as well. I can't tell you how many times I have missed elk sign because I failed to look for it. I had mentally written off the trail because I thought only cattle or sheep were using it.

Slopes

Though steep by human standards, slopes of 10 to 30 percent are little challenge to elk for grazing or travel. I remember glassing a herd of elk in south central Colorado some years back on a scouting trip in late July. Though daytime temperatures were reaching into the 70s°F (20s°C), there were still plenty of snow pockets trapped on northern slopes above 11,000 feet (3,352 m), and these elk were scattered over ¼ mile (0.4 km) of this particular slope, which in some places appeared to be as much as a 40 percent grade. All the while they were feeding and staying cool lying in the snow as if they were on level ground.

Research indicates that beyond about 30 percent,

Even on bare ground, elk migrate using The Law of Least Effort.

Elk have thick hides and do not perspire through it. A cool dip on a fall day helps regulate body temperature.

elk use usually drops off significantly, with little elk activity on slopes above 50 percent. However, the same research shows that elk use tends to increase with an increase in slope, with the highest frequency of use found on slopes in the 15 to 30 percent range. Had we tried to make our way up the slope to the elevation where the elk were, I seriously believe our lungs would have burst. For the elk, it was just routine. The point here is that just because the slope is tough on the hunter does not mean you won't find elk there.

During early fall when temps may still spike into the high 70s°F (20s°C), elk frequently use creek and drainage bottoms for travel routes because of the promise of water, high-quality forage and thermal cover from the heat of Indian summer days. Though difficult for the hunter to traverse because of the extreme density of cover found bordering such areas, hunters should not dismiss these travel routes.

Look for stands where you can observe these corridors, especially where they may open up near the heads of drainages. Also look for well-used trails emerging from dark timber that feed into these creek bottoms. In areas where you can actually find moving water, look for elk sign in the cutbacks in the creek where water pools and elk may come to drink, remaining under the cover of brush bordering the creek. While I am not a huge advocate of using tree stands for elk hunting, if you find a water source that is being frequented by elk, this would make for an excellent location for a stand.

Learning about Land and Travel Patterns from the Air

Having spent an entire career strapped to the seat of fighter jets in the Air Force, I have acquired a keen sense of the perspective one gains from looking over an area from altitude. While it is not for everyone, if you have the resources—and it's really not that expensive—take the opportunity to spend even a small amount of time flying over the area you plan to hunt. You'll learn more about that area and the general travel patterns of elk in one hour than you will in a month of scouting on the ground. Don't get me wrong on this. I am not saying that flying over your hunting area is a replacement for quality time spent scouting on the ground. What I am saying is that the bird's-eye view from the air provides you with information and perspective that you never get on the ground.

From the air, you gain an acute sense of the topography of the land that perhaps 1 percent of hunters can discern from a topo map. If you have a topo of the area with you in the aircraft, even better—what you see will help to clarify what the map is telling you. Make sure to take your GPS along on the flight to mark spots that may be of interest once you get back on the ground and begin hunting. In addition to learning how to access specific areas that you may want to hunt, well-used trails in open areas stand out clearly. In many cases numerous trails paralleling one another across a slope, indicating travel patterns, are evident. You will be able to see where these trails lead into dark timbered areas and where they come out on the opposite side. You will see which saddles are getting heavier use. Don't worry about seeing elk. That is not the objective. The overflight is to help you learn more about the area itself.

If you do happen to see elk, that's just icing on the cake.

Once the shooting begins, elk tend to head to areas that are difficult for hunters to access. From the air, say 3,000 to 5,000 feet (914 to 1,524 m) AGL (above the surrounding terrain), you will be able to look down into the bottom of some of those deep holes and cuts that you would never otherwise investigate, thus possibly missing out on a first-class elk area.

If you plan to do some flying over elk country, make sure to check out the local laws in this regard. Some states have regulations about the amount of time required between an overflight of an area and when you can actually begin hunting.

Because of the inherent difficulty of flying in mountainous terrain, it is critical that you never try to do this alone. Mountain flying in the Rockies is nothing like flying over flat farmland, and many a wayward pilot has failed to come home because he or she headed the craft into the mountains with little or no mountain flying training. It's much safer to hire the plane and a competent mountain-qualified pilot while you go along as the observer.

A view from the air can help you discern how the elk are using the area.

Chapter 3

FINE-TUNING YOUR CALLING

No other topic of discussion related to elk hunting is more openly debated than the value of calling elk. I, for one, am a strong advocate of the sensible (emphasis on sensible) use of elk calls, especially cow calls.

Elk are herd animals and, as such, have developed a social network that leans largely upon the use of active vocalization. Elk talk or effective calling can play a decisive role in the success of your elk hunting.

Cows and calves are talking among themselves all the time. Bulls, while not as vocal as cows, also vocalize, especially prior to and during the rut. The hunter who learns how to make a few basic cow calls can not only attract a love-sick bull, but can also use the call to cover inadvertent missteps during a stalk.

The hunter must be careful, however, not to call so much as to allow the bull or cow to get a fix on his position. Personally I quit calling once the elk in question is within 100 yards (91 m). After the bull closes to that range I see it as my responsibility to close the rest of the distance on my own.

As the number of hunters afield grows each year it is important to remember that not every elk call in the woods comes from a real elk.

Here is one of my favorite stories about this subject: It was sometime back in the early 1990s and I was hunting alone in the Gunnison area of Colorado. I was set up just below the crest of a ridgeline overlooking a couple of well-used game trails. About 50 yards (46 m) beyond the trails was an old grown-over Forest Service fire road.

Though rarely used by humans anymore, old fire roads criss-cross all over elk country. They make easier travel routes.

I had been in place for about an hour or so when I heard a cow calling from somewhere up the forest road to my left. So like any good elk hunter, I whipped out my trusty cow call and answered. Sure enough, she answered back. This conversation went on for a few minutes and I could tell that the cow was moving closer and closer. Finally I decided it was time to shut up and see what would happen rather than run the risk of getting busted.

Well, this cow started calling and calling and calling, like every five seconds, like she didn't have a friend in the world. Listening to this racket, it started to dawn on me that something might not be right, or at least not as right as it seemed. For the next couple of minutes all I heard was this cow, or what I had thought was a cow going off over and over. About that time,

the mystery became clear as two hunters on horseback came riding down that Forest Service road still hootin' like crazy on those cow calls—both of 'em! It must have taken these guys another five minutes to pass out of my range of hearing, and all that time they just kept hootin' on those cow calls.

Since that time, I have had the opportunity to listen to many elk—singles, small herds and large herds. By comparison, the only cow talk that has ever come close to the racket that those two hunters were making as they rode through the woods that day, has been the cow talk of medium to large herds of elk in the early summer when the calves are about and elk talk is everywhere. My point here is that if you are going to use an elk call, know how to use it and, more important, when to use it.

BUGLING VERSUS COW CALLS

Many "experts" say that the days of bugling in big bulls, while not extinct, are definitely on the decline. Over the years, mature bulls have learned not to trust the sounds that they once may have taken for those made by their own. To some extent this is probably true, in a very general sense. Not being an elk, I don't know what they think of them; all I see is how they react.

In many cases, however, the problem with bugles seems to be more of overuse and indiscriminate calling rather than focusing on one particular bull. I have had many positive encounters with bulls while using a bugle. Yet in every case, I was attempting to talk to one particular bull. Broadcast bugling is rarely effective, especially on highly pressured elk.

Prior to the heat of the rut, bulls eagerly respond to a cow call.

The only downside to using a mouth call is learning to use it. Unlike reed-type calls, which are almost fool-proof, diaphragms do require a bit of practice and some getting used to. Because diaphragms fit into the roof your mouth, some users tend to gag on them, which is a normal reaction to something large and foreign in your mouth. When I was first learning to use a mouth call, I had this same problem. Some people are prone to this reflex action, while others never notice it.

It didn't seem to make any difference if it was in the upper half of my mouth or the lower half. All that mattered was that because it was there, my brain began to adjust to its presence in my mouth.

Reed-type cow calls can be effective at any time during hunting season.

VALLEY SERENADE

I was sitting on a dark timbered hillside some years ago, a good hour before official sunrise, when the serenade began.

As I shifted my position, trying to burrow myself into the hillside in the hope that some measure of warmth might be hidden beneath the pine needles on the forest floor, a slow and low-pitched growl issued forth from the valley floor below, gradually building, growing higher and higher until I thought that whatever manner of beast that had made it would surely bust a gut before it was all over. As the bugle hit what I thought would be its high note, another began and then another until it seemed as if the entire valley had become some sort of natural orchestra.

I must admit that in all my years hunting, I had never before and have not since heard a more beautiful symphony. The bugling went on, nonstop, for what seemed like half an hour. Much of the time, I simply sat and listened with my eyes closed, imagining the elk singing to one another. When at last the orchestra ceased, I opened my eyes and beheld the eastern sky, which had turned away from the dark of night ushering in another day, as if the sun were called to rise up by the elk themselves.

The longer I left it there, the less I thought about it. The less I thought about it, the less the gag reflex. After a few minutes, I was able to move the call into place with my tongue at the front part of my palate. From time to time, early on, the gag reflex may come back. If it does, move the call back to the side of your mouth. Don't take it out all the way unless you think that you're going to swallow it. The longer you can leave the call in your mouth, the quicker you'll adjust and can then begin to use the call.

Jay's Tip

The key that I found to overcoming the gag reflex was to place the call in the side of my mouth outside of my teeth when it was not in use. This way my mouth got used to it being there.

Reed Calls

Reed-type calls are a great alternative to the mouth call, especially for new elk hunters. These calls are mostly barrel-type calls with a mouthpiece on the back end of the barrel and a Mylar or other synthetic reed inserted into the mouthpiece. Simply insert the mouthpiece about ½ inch (1.3 cm) into your mouth, bite down gently and blow. This action causes air to move over the surface of the reed, which then vibrates and produces a sound that is amplified through the barrel. You can control pitch and volume by the pressure on your bite (less pressure equals lower sounds, more bite pressure equals higher tones) and the amount of air pressure blowing through the call.

Because cow calls are less threatening than other types of calls, they often get a bull's attention quicker.

Reed calls, such as the Sceery Ace-1, will do the trick if you're well practiced.

Reed calls are very easy to learn to use. I use a number of cow calls, including Sceery's Ace-1, and Primos's Hyper Lip Single and Hoochie Mama. I've used many other cow calls and still do, but for the beginner, the Sceery Ace-1 is tough to beat. One of the best ways to learn to use either type of call is to purchase a CD or audiotape of elk calls, available from most suppliers, and then mimic those calls with your call.

Jay's Tip

Where you practice your calls is entirely up to you, but experience has taught many of us not to try this in the house. Unless you have a very, very understanding spouse when it comes to disturbing the peace in the home, try this in the car or truck on the way to or from work.

WHEN TO CALL

Remember the line in the old song "you've got to know when to hold 'em, know when to fold 'em"? If you want to be successful at calling elk, a similar rule applies: know when to call and when to be quiet. Elk are not all that different from us in the way they communicate with each other. Human communication is a two-way affair. If you say something to me or ask me a question, it provokes a response. In other words, for each action there is a reaction. If you start talking to me and I fail to respond, you may determine that I've lost interest and you probably stop talking. Elk behave similarly. Unless there are outside influences, they may carry on conversations throughout the day as long as someone is talking back, whether it is another cow, their calf, or someone that sounds like another elk.

My rule of thumb is, once I have established a conversation, keep talking. Keep the conversation going and keep the interest level up until the elk begins to move close enough to distinguish that you are not the real deal. How close is this? It depends on factors such as cover, terrain, weather, wind and so on. Consider all of the factors that would extend or reduce the elk's ability to determine whether the sound was a real elk or you.

Like talking to another human, suggestive calling tends to work better than aggressive calling. There are exceptions to this rule—calling bulls during the rut is one—but, overall, persuasion appears to work better. If you are working a bull that is all fired up during the rut, you may want to try to sound more aggressive,

Judicious and timely use of a call can really grab a bull's attention.

Bugling from a high point can be a good way of locating elk.

If you cause even one cow to be alarmed, the rest of the herd will likely scatter, too.

more in-your-face. Some bulls respond in kind and come charging toward the call, attempting to drive off a potential threat; this is especially true if the bull is a herd bull and you sound like a spike or immature bull that has just trespassed onto the herd bull's territory. On the other hand, the lead cow may gather him up and hightail it right out of there.

Aggressive calling is always risky, but it may be the only way to lure the bull your way. If you do manage to bring in one of these monsters, be ready! This is especially true for bowhunters who must wait until they almost can see the whites, or in some cases red, of the bull's eyes before taking a shot. Also think about having a large tree handy that you could get behind if that bad boy gets too close.

Finally, know when to be quiet. As mentioned above, once the elk is in close or you think that he may have located you, it's time to hush, get ready and keep your eyes open to any kind of movement. Remember the earlier story of the two guys on horseback hooting and hooting on their cow calls? While elk do talk considerably throughout the day, the same elk doesn't

talk every second. As with humans, too much talk can have an adverse reaction with elk.

Communication, whether with people or elk, is a balance of listening and responding. If you are ever fortunate enough to find yourself within hearing range of a herd of elk, take the time to listen to them for a while. I've done this many times, but my focus is usually on the hunting or learning to imitate the sounds of their talk. By listening to the conversations, we can learn not only the sounds, but also how the dialog plays out, the nuance of the communication process, even if we cannot understand it. If there are a lot of cows and calves, there will surely be a lot of conversation, but not all from the same elk.

Jay's Tip

Cow calling should resemble a persuasive conversation, not a contest to see who can talk the most or the loudest. It's about building a relationship. Think about talking to your spouse. Which works best, gentle persuasion or yelling? I think most of you will get the point.

Chapter 4

HUNTING WITH PROVEN STRATEGIES

As I mentioned earlier, elk country is "big country" and the tactics and strategies required for a successful hunt may be different from those used when hunting woodlots or pastures for whitetail in the Midwest or back East. You need to be prepared to cover as much territory as possible during the course of your hunt, as elk are almost always on the move seeking out highly nutritious forage for the upcoming winter. One day they may be in a particular drainage and the next day they have moved out in search of additional sources of food.

Most veteran elk hunters tell you that locating the elk in these vast expanses of wilderness is often the biggest challenge. While elk do tend to inhabit general ranges in summer and winter, where to find them within this area becomes the question of the day. This type of hunt requires a plan.

I grew up hunting whitetail in the South. The tactic there was to climb up in a tree and wait, for the entire season if necessary, until the deer came within gun or bow range. This strategy is very successful due to the dense deer populations in the South and the fact that whitetail travel as singles or small groups, thus spreading them out over a wide area. Okay, so now you know the difference between the way that elk travel and the way that deer travel. So how does one hunt these monsters called elk?

USING EFFECTIVE CAMOUFLAGE

Bowhunters have long known the inestimable value of wearing effective camouflage to gain an advantage in pursuit of wapiti. It has only been in the past 10 years or so, however, that significant numbers of rifle hunters have come to acknowledge this same truth. For years rifle hunters argued that since their shots would likely occur at longer ranges than those required of bowhunters, there was no need to go to the trouble and expense of buying camo hunting gear.

As many shot opportunities go during rifle season, I might agree with this argument were it not for those times, and we all know of them, when a fine bull or cow has popped up close and silent, catching the hunter off guard, with little cover in which to conceal his or her movement while preparing for the shot. As a result there stands the hunter, a big vertical, solid mass that looks and smells in every way to the elk . . . like a human. The elk's reaction? Swap ends and exit the country—now!

I have personally heard a few longtime rifle hunters say something to the effect of, "I don't need no cam-u-flage to kill an elk." Well, I agree; you don't. I have yet to witness or hear of an elk brought to ground by a set of camouflage. I do believe, however, that all else being equal, those elk hunters who choose to don camo appropriate for the season and surroundings are much more likely to sneak up on and whack a nice branch-antlered bull or a plump cow than those who do not.

Flight Response

Have you ever been convinced that you were busted when a bull or cow looked you dead in the eye from close range? Yet for some unexplained reason they continued to feed or go about their business. I have seen this behavior dozens of times in the field and on film as well. A videographer I know of recently produced a nice video with various scenes of one specific large bull elk. In more than one case, the bull curiously looked directly at the cameraman, but continued to graze, only occasionally glancing back in the direction of the camera.

My theory, and that of many of the elk biologists and professionals in the field, explains this unexpected behavior. It is what I like to call my "Two Strikes and You Are Out Theory."

The self-protection mechanism of elk depends primarily upon external input to their three primary senses: smell, hearing and vision. Because an elk's sense of smell has been so finely attuned to detect danger over thousands of generations, in the case of a snoot full of "man odor" elk may elect to trigger or flee with just this one sense receiving input. However, in situations where elk hear or see something unusual, I believe they may alert (show interest). With only one sensory input, they will likely not trigger (flee) until that initial sensory input is confirmed by input from a second self-defense sensory system. Two strikes and you are out.

For the bull that comes in silently, the hunter needs every advantage possible.

With just one whiff, a bull can detect something amiss. If confirmed by a second sense, he may disappear from sight.

Color Vision in Elk

Before we go too far down the road on the value of camouflage, here is something to think about that may persuade you to gear up in a set of camo next time you head out to elk country. At the very least it may cause you to rethink the duds that you hunt in.

Recent research shows that, contrary to much popular opinion of the past, white-tailed deer—and likely by ancestral association their cervid cousin, the elk—possess the anatomical requisites (cones) for color vision and do in fact discern a limited range of colors.

Since this discussion challenges conventionally held wisdom on deer and elk vision, I want to make it clear that the sources of the research that support this conclusion are from well respected, peer-reviewed individuals and studies in the scientific community and not merely from the personal experience of one or more individuals. Most of the empirical work discussed here was accomplished on deer. However, I personally interviewed three state and federal terrestrial elk biologists and several state wildlife officials who agree that the conclusions of this research on deer very likely apply to elk as well.

Elk depend on three senses for defense: smell, sight, and sound. Threat detection through smell usually triggers a flight response. If detection is via one of the other senses and the hunter can avoid a second confirming method, the elk may not flee.

In their study, "A Review of Color Vision in White-Tailed Deer" (Wildlife Society Bulletin, 2003), Kurt C. VerCauteren and Michael J. Pipas state that "during the day deer [elk] discriminate colors in the range blue to yellow-green and can also distinguish longer (orange-red) wavelengths. At night deer [elk] see color in the blue to blue-green range." This sensitivity to the blue to blue-green portion of the spectrum peaks in low-light situations, such as predawn and late evening or twilight periods. These are traditionally popular times to hunt.

VerCauteren and Pipas further conclude, "Although deer [elk] can visually detect the color orange, it is the brightness [luminescence] of the fluorescent clothing worn by hunters and not the color per se that most likely draws a deer's [elk's] attention. Those who must approach . . . close [to] deer [elk] without being detected should not wear bright or contrasting clothing, and must respect the deer's [elk's] other senses (hearing, smell) at least equally."

Hunters are required to wear some amount of fluorescent orange during many elk hunting seasons. The experts I interviewed suggested that the brightness of such clothing can be reduced by wearing fluorescent orange made from softer materials like cotton or wool, rather than harder or more slick vinyl, plastic or synthetic materials, which are more luminescent or reflective.

Camo for the West

Until recently there were few commercial camo patterns that worked well for elk hunting in the West. Most of the readily available patterns were designed to realistically mimic eastern hardwoods or marshlands. In my experience these patterns don't meet the needs of elk hunters who hunt low to the ground (rarely in a tree stand), above timberline, often in shady dark pine timber, on open rocky talus or sage-covered slopes or in juniper brush—or in all of the above.

The purpose of camouflage is to break up the human outline and allow the hunter to become visually less distinguishable from the surroundings. In the course of any hunt we may encounter a variety of environments, so we need to ensure that our camo doesn't create a problem rather than solve one.

For example, if you are hunting above timberline on a rocky or grass-covered slope while wearing a dark forest-type camo pattern, you will stand out from the background rather than blend into it. Conversely, you will encounter a similar problem while hunting dark timber in a light-colored pattern.

So what is the solution? Consider two sets of camo. I typically carry one of each to elk camp, a dark set for black timber and a very generic lighter set for hunting open ground, because I don't know from day to day what type of ground I will be hunting. Some of you are bound to ask, do I come back to camp and change during the day or carry the other set in my daypack? Well I have been accused of being a bit on the picky side, but I'm not that picky. In most cases I do not go to this extreme unless I find myself back in camp for other reasons.

When it's time to purchase that next set of camo, consider the type of terrain and cover predominant in the areas you hunt. If you hunt higher elevations where the elk are often found during pre-rut and the rut, you may find that you are hunting above timberline a lot and need a pattern that works well in the open and on rocky slopes. In this environment, patterns that resemble hardwoods or marshes could even work against you. What you need is an open pattern of generic shapes that includes a mixture of muted shades of gray and green to help you blend in with sage, cactus and rocks.

Effective camo helps the hunter blend into the landscape, even in the open.

The Sitka Gear pattern is an example of camo that works well in dark timber and open terrain.

Hard-working camo keeps you out of sight.

Late morning and midday when the elk have moved out of their feeding areas and back into the black timber to bed down can be, in my opinion, some of the most productive times to hunt. Rather than being on the move from one area to another, elk are more sedentary during these midday hours as they rest and digest. When hunting densely forested areas and blowdowns, consider using a darker, more 3-D camo pattern that blends in well in a pine-type environment that is dominated by shadows and deadfalls.

To better understand my point, try to visualize this scene, which I saw about a year ago while watching a video produced by the manufacturer of a scent cover-up product: A rather nervous bowhunter, covered from head to toe in camo and presumably a host of scent containment systems, is kneeling behind a fallen log. His trusty bow is right there in his hand, but alas the hunter is as fixed as a marble statue incapable of movement. Why? Well almost certainly because a monster bull elk is standing over the hapless hunter at what appears to be less than 2 feet (60 cm) with his nose about 6 inches (15 cm) from the poor bowhunter's left ear. Strike one.

This business of the bull elk trying to determine who or what this funny looking animal behind the

log is continues for what seems like minutes. To his credit—and possibly his longevity—the hunter remains completely motionless throughout most of this encounter. Surely his thoughts during this "time of trial" are less on whether or not he will be successful in his hunting efforts, and more on whether or not he will make it through the event with clean shorts or even if he will survive the day. After what seems to the viewer like a very prolonged engagement between the bull and the bowhunter, it appears that the hunter could no longer stand the strain and moves just a hair. Strike two! The bull immediately detects this ever-so-slight movement and does a one-eighty and hightails it for parts unknown.

Clearly in this situation the bull could see the hunter; otherwise why would he have continued to indulge his interest for so long? But without additional clues from his other senses—motion, sound or scent— the hunter remained merely a curiosity. Once the bull's vision sense picked up a second clue, movement, the bull's self-preservation mechanism kicked into gear. Putting one and one together made for strike two. The bull recognized the hunter for what he was, a potential threat, and the bull triggered or reacted accordingly.

RUN AND GUN

Sometimes known as "spot-and-stalk," this tactic involves identifying a number of prominent or high spots from which you can glass a fairly large piece of real estate with binoculars. This might be a ridge fingertip, a clear-cut, a south-facing hillside or a rock outcropping overlooking a draw. Any position that allows you to visually inspect a large tract of land will do.

Because of the great line-of-sight distances that may be involved in this process—anywhere from a few hundred yards (m) to perhaps miles (km)—it is important to bring along a pair of first-class optics and a bucket load of patience. Now you may be saying to yourself, Patience? Me? Who is this guy kidding? I can't even spell patience, much less maintain any. Remember the old cartoon of two vultures sitting on a limb and one says to the other, "Patience, heck, I want to kill something." You can! When it comes to sitting and waiting, I am the least patient person I know. At the grocery store, if the lines are too long, I'm the guy who just puts it back on the shelf and comes back another time rather than wait in line. But when it comes to elk hunting and all the time, effort and expense that I have put into a hunt over the course of a year, I learn to practice patience—at least for a week. If I can do it, you can do it.

When to Move

That could be a lot of glassing, you may say. You bet it is. Think of it this way: That trophy bull you're seeking is hiding out there somewhere, maybe bedded down behind that lone juniper, perhaps standing facing away from you just on the edge of that clear-cut. He is the pot of gold at the end of the rainbow, and the reason you are here. Why would you shortcut your pursuit because you get tired of looking? Elk hunting is not convenient, and it's not easy or for the faint of heart. If it were, the statistics showing an average success ratio of 1:8 (one successful elk hunt every eight years) would not hold true. If you want to score every time you go out, go shoot some tin cans.

Jay's Tip

Just how long do you need to be out there? The answer here is, as long as it takes to glass absolutely every single inch (cm) of ground that can be seen with your binoculars or "Mark One" eyeball.

Glassing helps a hunter cover a lot of ground in a relatively short time. Look for movement, trails, signs of passage, and bedding or travel routes.

When you are glassing, you need to look for parts of the elk. It's not often that you see an entire bull or cow elk standing in the open like on a magazine cover, with a sign nearby saying "shoot here." No, most elk spotted in this manner are located by noticing things that appear out of the ordinary, like the horizontal line of an elk's back when nature produces mostly vertical lines. Or it could be a momentary glint of sunlight bouncing off an antler, or the tan patch of an elk's backside against the backdrop of green timber. Look for parts, movement, anything that may indicate the presence of the elk. Believe me, this is not easy. We have all read the magazines and watched the videos or cable channel images of elk that become branded on our mind's eye. It is only natural when we go looking for elk that we look for the entire beast. Training your eye to look for elk parts takes some work and focus, but you can do it.

Once you're sure that you have glassed the entire area, consider doing it again. During the early morning and late evening hours, elk are constantly on the move, either to or from bedding areas, and in this travel they may move through the area that you are glassing.

While you are glassing, consider using your call. You'll be surprised how far the sound of a bugle or cow call carries from such an unobstructed point, especially if used with a grunt tube to direct or amplify the call. Many successful elk hunters can attest that this is a great way to locate elk.

If, after thoroughly glassing an area and trying your call a few times in the process, you have not seen any elk or had any replies to your call, it is time to pick up your gear and head to the next similar spot that you scouted before heading in that day. Remember, always have a plan for the day. This allows you to cover the most ground in the least amount of time and prevents you from just wandering around elk country in circles. Use your topo map and compass or GPS to help you move from point to point.

Highly pressured elk often will only leave the cover of timber in the last few moments before dark.

A bull's sense of smell is his Number One defense.

Stalking Factors

Okay, what if you do see that 6 × 6 bull or hear cows talking from your lofty perch, what do you do now? Here is where you have to get smart and commit—the stalk. It's time to reach way down inside to that hunter-gatherer embedded deep within your DNA and come alive. It's right now that you need to take into account all the factors that may affect the outcome of your stalk.

Factor #1: Wind. The first factor to consider is the wind. While your high school geometry teacher may have taught you that the shortest distance between two points (you and the elk) is a straight line, there is a better than average chance that this straight line isn't going to work for your stalk. You would be surprised by how many times hunters do just that. They see or hear a bull and unthinkingly move directly for the animal without considering the effects of the wind.

An elk's sense of smell is its number one defense against a predator, and like it or not, that's exactly what we as elk hunters are—predators. One whiff of an elk hunter, whether it's from the bacon and eggs that you ate for breakfast stinking up your gear or from that bar of soap you used last night, it doesn't smell right to elk and they will be gone like a shot if they wind you. Before beginning your stalk, develop a plan that takes the wind into account. If this means, and it does more often than not, that you have to plan a circuitous route around the elk to approach them from a more favorable wind direction, then that is what you have to do.

Factor #2: Geography. Many times this type of stalk requires you to walk much farther than a direct approach would have and to cover some pretty nasty terrain. This is where your level of commitment will be measured.

Elk feed—and may even bed down—on small benches, which are flat areas on a hillside. A trained eye can locate these benches on a topo map during pre-hunt scouting.

Factor #3: Commitment. Ideally, you would have asked and answered these questions before you left home, but many times the real test of commitment that can lead to a successful elk hunt comes right here. It is time to fish or cut bait. Are you in or out? Sure you are . . . made the decision . . . I am ready. I will do it . . . this is why I am here.

While you are making your stalk, keep in mind that the wind changes all the time in elk country, especially in canyons where it can swirl all over the place. Use your wind checker regularly as you proceed, to make sure that you either stay downwind of the elk or have some type of terrain between you and the elk to keep your scent from reaching them if you need to be upwind for a time.

Jay's Tip

As a rule, it is usually better to approach from above, that is, uphill of the elk.

This is true for a number of reasons, especially if you are hunting during the middle of the day. First, during late morning and midday the heating of the earth forces the warm air to rise and move from lower elevations to higher elevations, or uphill. Second, when elk bed on hillsides, they tend to orient themselves facing downhill or into the wind. Finally, it is my experience that more often than not, when shot at or alarmed, elk tend to run uphill. This last tip is not a guarantee, just an observation, so don't go running off and telling your hunting buddies that elk always run uphill when shot at. As sure as you do, you or someone is going to miss a shot and that elk is going to run straight downhill and you have some explaining to do.

STAND HUNTING

Stand hunting in elk country is usually limited to hunting over water holes or wallows. Wallows can be anything from a spring to a seep, or even a small pond-like body of water. Elk frequent these for drinking water and also to help cool their bodies. Wallows vary in size from just a few feet (m) in diameter to as much as 20 feet (6.1 m) or so across. Some may be filled with muddy water (a good sign that it is in use), while others may only hold the mud. Frequently used wallows show plenty of elk sign in the way of tracks, muddy water and trails leading into and out of the area. Heavily frequented wallows are excellent locations for setting up a stand.

Stand-Hunting Factors

Stand hunting over wallows can require even more patience than the run-and-gun approach, as you must sit very still and quiet for long periods of time. Here are three factors that may influence where you place your stand over a wallow.

Factor #1: Clear Shooting Lanes. Position your stand so you have a number of unobstructed directions of fire, as it is difficult to predict from which direction the elk will approach the wallow. The key here is to give yourself as much flexibility as possible.

Factor #2: Wind. It's important to determine the prevailing wind direction near the wallow and factor this into your plan to keep your scent from drifting toward the wallow or the approaches the elk might choose to use. Okay, you ask, what if there are trails leading to the wallow from all directions?

Try to determine which trail or trails are being used the most and focus on these. There are no guarantees that you'll pick the right one; just use your best judgment.

Some hunters place game cameras near a wallow to snap photos of the game automatically as they come in. If your checkbook can handle it, these tools can provide clues on which elk are using the wallow and how they approach it.

Factor #3: Cover. Try to use natural cover to your advantage. Since wallows are often found in smaller clearings surrounded by timber, as opposed to out in the middle of a meadow, there is a good chance that your encounter with the elk will be at close range. Movement or sound that may go unnoticed by elk at long range will almost always light their afterburners from close range.

When hunting from a stand, I recommend the use of good camouflage, including a head mask, so that the elk see your form and minor movements as just another part of the landscape.

Ultimately, many factors affect the success of your elk hunt. Whether you choose the run-and-gun method, stand hunting over a wallow or a combination thereof is up to you and the movement of the elk in your area. Whichever method you choose, have a plan and execute it.

Normally, elk hunting requires covering a lot of ground. Sometimes, however, as is the case with a well-used wallow, stand hunting can be productive.

WAIT-TIME AFTER A SHOT

How long should you wait after the shot to pursue your animal, especially if you're a bowhunter? Elk are large-bodied animals that in most cases run only a short distance after being shot, whether with a rifle or bow, before stopping to assess their situation. By this I don't mean to imply that they think it through, but more that their instinctive response is to flee the immediate area where they encountered a threat. Once clear—and this may be as few as 50 yards (46 m) or so—if left alone and not pursued, they slow down or stop.

I like to cow call following the shot as a way to help a wounded animal settle down. The tendency of most hunters that I have known or met is to wait a few minutes and then set off in pursuit of their trophy. Each situation is different, but I can say with assurance that the hunter who pursues a shot elk prematurely is not going to get him to crash any sooner. Think about it, if someone had shot you and was chasing you with a gun or bow, would you stop to see what was going to happen?

Here are my rules of thumb for how long to wait:

- If the bull goes down right in front of me like he was pole-axed, I give him 30 minutes before I move in his direction.
- If he runs out of sight following the shot, but I am certain that he is hit hard in both lungs or the heart, I wait anywhere from 1 to 3 hours.
- Finally, if there is any question in my mind—*any*—especially when bowhunting, that the shot was not a double lung or heart shot, I wait 8 or more hours before pursuing the animal, the idea being to give the elk the opportunity to lie down and expire.

When hit, the animal's body begins to flood with adrenaline to support the fight-or-flight mechanism. Think of adrenaline as nitrous oxide, a fuel additive for race cars that when injected into the fuel stream substantially increases their horsepower and speed almost instantaneously. Once the adrenaline hits, the animal uses this increased fuel and horsepower to put as much distance between it and the threat it perceives, until either the fuel runs out or it no longer perceives the threat. I have heard stories of more animals lost forever because the hunter could not wait to get on the move to see what he had shot, and the animal kept moving, though mortally wounded, for miles (km). Patience is the key.

New-growth areas are ripe for elk grazing

Water, even deep water, is not a deterrent to elk travel.

The right camouflage and a good partner can make or break a hunt.

Chapter 5

MAKING A GREAT ELK CAMP

In his exceptional book, *Elk and Elk Hunting,* Hart Wixom shares with us, "a successful elk hunter can be told by the camp he keeps." This chapter provides a few pointers that will help you put together a first-class elk camp.

Elk hunting is so much more than the actual time spent hiking high-country bowls and trudging through deep snows or nasty blowdowns in search of wapiti. Though the average elk hunter may think of "the hunt" as the focal point of his or her efforts, most agree that it is also a time of fellowship and camaraderie, of nourishment and rest for our weary souls and worn-out bodies.

While a dusty wall tent heated by a fussy wood stove and filled with sleeping bags, boots drying by the stove, and piles of assorted gear may not seem like "Home Sweet Home" to most, to an elk hunter it just doesn't get any better. This is where the plans of the day are hatched and tales of close encounters are regaled. Depending on the sleeping habits of your fellow hunters, a good pair of earplugs is strongly advised.

The cook tent is the equivalent of the town square where everyone gathers to share, reminisce, and fill his or her belly. A steaming cup of cowboy coffee is the drink of the day. Author's note: Seasoned elk hunters know better that to drink the last few sips from your cup or anything near the bottom of the pot.

Here are some ways to make life in elk camp more hospitable.

MY TWO-BAG CLOTHING PLAN

Every year thousands of elk hunters wonder what gear they should take to elk camp. Most want to know how to prepare for the many possible contingencies that may occur as a result of the finicky weather in the Rockies. If you have ever hunted the high country, you know that a typical day of elk hunting may start out long before dawn with frosty single-digit temperatures. By noon the weather can require sunscreen and even shorts, or just as easily you could be overrun with freezing rain or blowing snow. Such is the nature of elk hunting. So how do you prepare for such extremes in the weather?

Since the amount of gear that one can store at elk camp is limited, over the years I have devised what I call my two-bag system. When I start gathering my gear for elk camp I pack two bags, one for the weather that I most expect to encounter—mild weather where temperatures may dip as low as 30°F (-1°C) during the day, since I usually hunt between mid-September and mid-October—and another smaller bag for my colder weather gear. If you are a late-season hunter and expect to spend a lot of time in deep snow and below-freezing temps, then forget the smaller bag. All you need is one large bag filled with cold weather gear.

Packing into a remote camp with a professional outfitter may offer the greatest opportunity for success.

A well-planned and organized camp can make the difference between a miserable outing and a great hunt.

A small, well-heated mountain cabin makes an excellent high-country elk camp!

My cold weather bag contains the following:

- An extra set of well broken-in boots lined with Gore-Tex or some other waterproofing material and insulated with 1,000 grams of Thinsulate
- A quiet insulated waterproof camo parka
- A heavier set of thermal long johns
- An extra set of insulated gloves
- Heavier poly/wool socks
- A bucket load of those chemical heat packs
- A folding camo flexible stadium seat

Stadium seat? Yep, these little gems can make all the difference if you're hunting in rain or snow or sitting on a pitched hillside. They save wear and tear on your back and keep your backside dry as well. They are simple seats with a sewn hinge connecting the seat and back, with adjustable nylon straps on either side to control the angle of the back. While stadium seats can be found in almost any sporting goods store in a variety of bright colors, mine is a camo version.

A QUALITY AND ROOMY TENT

Good, hearty food and a warm cook tent is a welcome sight after a long day's hunt.

For years I used an assortment of small, lightweight pop-up tents mainly because they were cheap and didn't take up much room in my vehicle while hauling them to elk camp. As I have grown older, I have become weary of tripping over bodies in the middle of the night when nature inevitably calls—and I assure you once you pass forty this is going to happen. You'll find yourself stooping and hopping around to get dressed in frosty pre-dawn hours or having to sleep on a hard, cold ground pad because the tent is not big enough to accommodate a decent cot for your bedroll. Prior to the 2000 elk season, I made one of the best decisions of my hunting career. I purchased a roomy 12-foot × 14-foot (3.7 × 4.3 m) cotton canvas outfitter wall tent; since then, elk camp has never been the same.

Outfitter Tent

That first outfitter tent slept five hunters very comfortably and we could squeeze another two in if we had to. With five hunters, each had more than enough personal space to be comfortable for a week's worth of hunting and then some. Even with a wood stove or propane tank and heater to keep the chill off, there was still plenty of room. The ridgepole running the length of the tent made an excellent support from which a clothesline could be suspended for drying out those wet duds after a long day of hunting. Toss in a few sturdy cots with egg-crate foam for mattresses, some old carpet for a floor and you are set.

Some outfitters offer a very large camp site, with multiple buildings.

Unlike most of the smaller imported tents found in discount stores, a quality outfitter tent is constructed from heavy-duty 10- to 15-ounce (283 to 425 g) 100 percent cotton canvas. Cotton canvas tents are more durable than tents made from synthetic materials, insulate better and can be sealed without having to go to the time, expense and mess of applying seam sealer. One of the distinctive attributes of cotton canvas is that when it gets wet, the individual fibers swell and then shrink, drawing the weave of the material even tighter. This swelling fills in not only the gaps between the individual threads but also the holes left by the needle when the tent was constructed.

To precondition your cotton tent, the tent must be wet down thoroughly. I mean soaked. The easiest way to do this is to set the tent up, guying out the sides, the front end and the back end, and stake down the base. If you don't guy the sides, the roof may sag and water may collect above the eaves, causing the frame to collapse under the additional weight. Before wetting down the tent, remember to zip or tie the door shut. If the front corners of the tent are guyed out too tightly toward the sides, the zipper door may not operate smoothly.

Haul out the garden hose and soak the tent thoroughly, making sure to wet all surfaces and seams, and then allow it to dry completely. Check the tent often to make sure it is not straining or sagging. Once the tent is dry, repeat the entire process.

Every time I get a new tent, we go through this procedure. If you wait for a warm sunny day, you can usually complete the process in one day if you start early enough. If you are using a freestanding frame, be sure to allow your tent to dry thoroughly on the frame before putting it away. Check the material where it comes into contact with the frame to make sure it is completely dry. This is usually the last area to dry. Never put a damp tent into storage. If you do, you run the very real risk of the tent mildewing. Mildew is extremely destructive to cotton fabrics and can ruin your tent in short order if allowed to remain on the fabric.

Most tent manufacturers offer a choice of fabrics for your tent. Typically these involve a selection of

Not all glassing and scouting need be done on the ground. An elevated spotting stand can increase your chances of seeing elk.

A 6x6 is success!

Game bags should be elevated beyond the reach of other animals while awaiting pack-out at the end of the hunt. Place them farther out on a limb if there are bears in the area.

fabric weights (more weight equals more insulation and a longer fabric life), a flame retardant treatment and a mildew resistant treatment. All of my tents are ordered with all the above options. The peace of mind is worth the extra cost.

Granted, an outfitter tent may cost more up front, but over the long run you will come out far ahead if you take care of your tent. A canvas tent provides many more years of reliable service than most synthetic tents. It keeps you warmer and dryer, and since most are larger than the average discount store model, your accommodations will be far less crowded.

Jay's Tip

One last tip on tents: If there is even the most remote chance that you may encounter snow at elk camp, take along a plastic tarp large enough to create a tent fly. Even the most water-resistant materials can leak if snow is allowed to remain on the roof for a prolonged period. A plastic tent fly helps to ensure a dry stay at elk camp.

HEAT SOURCES

During elk season, daytime temps in the high country can range from below freezing to well into the 70s°F (20s°C). You can bet that when the sun goes down, those numbers are going to head south fast.

When it comes to managing the temperature inside the tent, you have basically three options: your own body heat, wood heat and propane heat.

Body Heat

One option is trying the Jeremiah Johnson thing—doing nothing and just gutting it out in what could be a long night in subzero temps. Take it from someone who

has tried this more than once when I was much younger, this is not a good idea, and can quickly take most if not all of the fun out of your hunt. Elk hunting is hard work and requires getting a good night's rest so your body can regenerate and get ready for the rigors of the next day's hunt. If you spend the night trying to keep from freezing your buns off, how much rest do you think you are going to get?

Wood Heat

Your second option is to purchase a good wood-burning stove and bring in a good supply of well-dried split

Wood stoves are the typical sources of heat in a high-country camp. To keep the tent warm requires everyone to help with the wood cutting chore.

wood for fuel. There are many quality models to choose from that can be purchased in the $200–$400 range. Wood-burning stoves are excellent sources of heat and many have optional accessories for heating and retaining hot water for washing up or coffee.

Jay's Tip

If you plan to bring in wood from your home state, you will want to investigate whether or not the state in which you will be hunting has regulations restricting the import of out-of-state wood due to possible infestations.

As far as fuel goes, burning hardwood is better if you have access to it, as it does not produce as much creosote in the flue as softer woods like pine and cedar. Creosote is a black tar-like substance that is a byproduct of burning many types of wood. Creosote can build up quickly in the flue and can obstruct your stove ventilation, making life in the tent fairly unpleasant if not unbearable. If you find your flue is not venting properly—a good sign is a bunch of smoke in the tent— carefully remove the flue from the stove via the roof hole,

after it has cooled, and try cleaning it out by tamping it on the ground or running a long branch with leaves down the pipe. If you're burning soft wood like pine for more than 8 hours in any 24-hour period, be aware that creosote can build up in a matter of days.

Most woodstoves are built tough, but one thing they are not built to do is feed themselves. In order to generate all that heat throughout long, cold high-country nights, you must either lay in a good load of hardwood or someone must draw the short straw and assume the duty of getting up around 2 a.m. to feed and stoke the fire. Now don't ask me why you have to do this at such a forsaken hour. There doesn't appear to be any rhyme or reason to how long these stoves stay hot. I have fired them up as early as 7 p.m. and as late as 10 p.m. and for some unexplained reason, they all seem to want to die out around 2 a.m. Why 2 a.m.? I guess it's because that is when it seems to be the coldest. As the guy who has "had the duty," let me tell you, the last thing you want to do when it is freezing in the tent is to crawl out of your sleeping bag and walk barefoot across the dirt tent floor or plastic tarp to try your hand at re-lighting a near-dead fire in the middle of the night.

THINGS THAT GO BOOM IN THE NIGHT

The third day of elk season had come and gone and by 8 p.m. I was dead tired, so I headed for the bunk tent right after supper. I crawled into my sleeping bag and quickly drifted off.

"The urge" struck around 2 a.m., snapping me from my restful bliss and nagging me until I decided to do something about it. I hauled myself out of a toasty sleeping bag and took care of business. Upon returning to the tent, I crossed over to the woodstove to see if there was any life left in it.

I saw that there wasn't the slightest sign of heat, so being the good guy and thinking of the welfare of my fellow hunters who were still fast asleep, I gathered up some of our special "pre-treated" kindling. An old outfitter had showed us how to keep our kindling stored in an old coffee can about half filled with diesel fuel. Since diesel has a low flash point it burns gradually when lit.

I suppose we had run out of our special diesel supply, and someone decided to refill our kindling coffee can with white gas. At 2 a.m. in a freezing-cold, pitch-dark tent, I was unaware of this little change that had been made to our fire starter. So I tossed a few pieces of "special" kindling into the stove and piled a load of split cordwood on top for good measure. I then struck a common 3-inch (7.6 cm) kitchen match and tossed it beneath a piece of the kindling in hopes of bringing some respite from the cold into our cozy little abode.

Well, as you can guess, the fire lit off all right, just not as I expected. With a *whoomp* that was heard clear across camp and a flash of striking brilliant orange flame that was probably picked up by the National Reconnaissance Office's satellites in space as some missile launch from Colorado, our little woodstove came to life. For that matter, so did every living creature within a few hundred yards (m) of our camp.

Fortunately, I was standing just far enough to the side of the opening to avoid becoming the feature attraction of a barbecue. Whew, guess I was living right that day!

In truth, woodstoves are the most commonly used source of heat for large tents and have been for decades. When used correctly, they keep the chill off for most of the night.

Managing the challenges of long days and cold nights are quickly forgotten when a trophy elk comes within range.

Propane Heat

The third option for staying warm through the night, and my personal preference by far, is a propane-fueled radiant heater. Depending on the model you choose, these can produce anywhere from 3,000 to 45,000 BTUs of heat. As long as you have propane and you are not somewhere above the Arctic Circle, you will stay warm.

The smaller units, like Coleman's PowerCat, run on a single 1-pound (.45 kg) disposable bottle of propane. I have used one of these to heat smaller two- to five-man pop-up tents. A single 1-pound (.45 kg) bottle of propane keeps the heater fired up for approximately 8 hours. If you light it off about 15 minutes before everyone turns in, these smaller tents will be toasty when it's time to hit the sack and it will keep the chill off in all but the most extreme nighttime temps. These

can be picked up in most major hunting and fishing stores for around $70.

The next step up from Coleman is the Mr. Heater Portable Buddy heater. This unit has two settings (low and high) and can produce up to 9,000 BTUs of heat on a 1-pound (.45 kg) bottle of propane. Since it is capable of producing more heat, it burns fuel at a faster rate and may only last 6 hours on a single bottle. This unit weighs about 10 pounds (4.5 kg) and can be purchased for around $80.

For those using large wall tents, you need a bit more horsepower to stay warm throughout the night. I use a three-burner-type propane radiant heater that mounts to the top of a conventional 20-pound (9 kg) bottle of propane. Each burner can be controlled individually, allowing me to produce anywhere from 6,000 BTUs to 45,000 BTUs. Some may ask, what setting is enough? Let me tell you, if you crank this heater full up to 45K BTUs in a 12 × 14 wall tent at temps anywhere above 0°F (-17.8°C), it will run you out of the tent in no time.

Here is how I use propane: For an average night with temps projected to drop to 15°F (-9°C), I fire up all three burners on their minimum setting about 15 minutes before everyone plans to retire. This makes for a very comfortable environment in which to change out of our hunting duds and into whatever we plan on sleeping in. Once everyone is tucked in, I turn off all but one burner that I leave on a mid-level setting (around 9,000 BTUs) for the remainder of the night. This usually is sufficient to keep the tent warm throughout the night. If I wake up and it's a bit chilly, all I have to do is turn up that single burner to get as much as 15,000 BTUs. I have hunted with this setup when the nighttime temps dropped as low as 0°F (−18°C) and have never had to light a second burner to keep the tent warm. Using a heater in this manner, you can expect to stay comfortable for five to six nights on a single 20-pound (9 kg) bottle of propane. Since you never know what the weather is going to be like in elk country, I always carry a spare 20-pound (9 kg) bottle of propane just in case a storm blows in and we get stuck in the tent for a few days.

If you elect to use a propane heater inside your tent, there is one warning that you should note. Just like any heater that burns fuel to produce heat, it requires oxygen to keep the burner lit. Where does it get the oxygen? From inside the tent of course. Be sure the tent is ventilated adequately to bring fresh air in and replenish the oxygen supply in the tent. Under normal conditions, enough oxygen makes its way into a tent to sustain all those inside; however, these type of heaters consume significantly more oxygen. Leave a window cracked or chimney flue flap open to provide some air circulation and avoid carbon monoxide poisoning.

KNOW YOUR TENT

I had purchased a brand-new tent from a major outdoor gear supplier and was eager to try it out, so my hunting partner and I hauled it to elk camp that year. This tent was my next step up from those small pop-ups and I could hardly wait to get it set up and see all the room that it would provide. We arrived at camp on a picture-perfect blue-sky 55°F (13°C) Thursday prior to the opening of Colorado's first rifle season the following Saturday.

Three of the requirements I had when purchasing this new tent was that it would be watertight, have plenty of room for up to four hunters and have a built-in floor.

It was unseasonably warm so I left one of the zip-up windows cracked for fresh air during the night. On the third day of the season, as can be the case in Colorado, a storm front moved through and the weather changed dramatically. Blue skies were exchanged for rain and light snow, and nighttime temps dropped into the low 30s (around -1°C). After hunting hard for three days, my partner and I had driven into Gunnison, Colorado, to treat ourselves to a steak dinner and a bit of civilization that evening. Upon our return to camp, it was raining cats and dogs so we quickly ducked into the tent, fired up the propane heater and drifted off to sleep with everything zipped up tight to keep out the rain.

About midnight I woke up short of breath and hearing the sound of water hitting the floor. Once the fog of sleep cleared, I looked over at the heater and saw it burning a dull cobalt blue instead of the normal red. Quickly I realized that because the tent was sealed up so tight, the heater was unable to draw air from outside and was consuming much of the oxygen in our tent. I hopped out of my sleeping bag into a puddle of water and unzipped the tent door about 12 inches (30 cm). Immediately the heater went from blue to its normal red and I began to feel better, all the while my hunting partner was sleeping through the whole event never knowing how close we may have come to tragedy.

Once the more critical issue was taken care of, I grabbed my flashlight to see where all the water was coming from. Much to my surprise and disappointment, almost every seam in my brand-new tent was leaking water from the storm outside. The only dry spot in the tent was directly under the peak of the roof where the pitch was enough to keep the water from coming in. I woke my hunting partner up and we spent the next half hour moving our gear into the only dry area of the tent where we slept until morning. With more wet and stormy weather on the way and a leaky tent, we decided to call off the remainder of the hunt and head home.

The lesson learned here is that we did not get the right instruction at purchase time. Looking back on this event, I now do thorough research on any product I buy. This way I don't have to rely on the opinion of a salesperson.

SLEEPING BAG

Shortchanging yourself by arriving at elk camp with an inadequate sleeping bag is one of the quickest ways I know of to wreck what would otherwise be a great hunting trip.

Temperature Rating

When you come to elk camp, I strongly advise bringing a quality sleeping bag that is rated to at least 0°F (-18°C). Unless you plan to hunt one of the later seasons in deep snow, such a bag should keep you warm in most situations. As most folks who have hunted the high country can attest, weather in the Rockies can and will change on a moment's notice.

Early in the 2004 elk season, an unexpected snowstorm that dropped nighttime temps from the low 40s°F to the low 20s°F (4.4° to -6.7°C) hammered many bowhunters in Colorado. According to eyewitness accounts, one minute the temperature was near 70°F (21°C) with beautiful clear skies, and two hours later the temps had dropped 35 degrees and snow was blowing

sideways. The lesson here is to be prepared for the worst weather that you expect to encounter. You can always crawl out of a bag that is too warm, but take it from one who has been there, you cannot crawl down deep enough into a bag that doesn't have enough insulation. Hunt smart!

Shape and Fill

Sleeping bags generally come in one of two types, conventional rectangular bags and mummy-style bags. If you are a large-framed guy like me (6-foot-3/183 cm and 230 pounds/104 kg), you will appreciate the roominess of an oversized conventional rectangular bag. Though definitely not designed for backpacking, these bags offer plenty of room in which one can toss and turn in exchange for the extra weight and bulk. For those who prefer lighter weight or more technical gear, mummy-style bags are the way to go. Also, mummy bags require less time to warm up since they have less space inside.

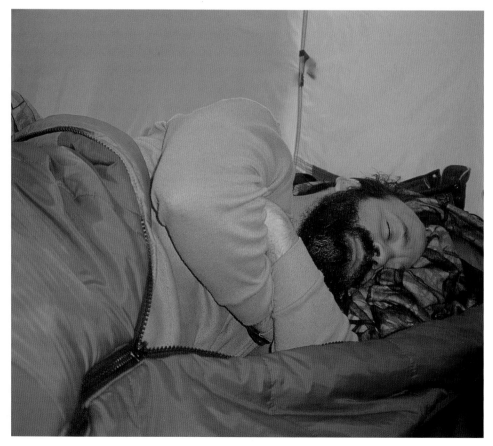

A mediocre sleeping bag usually makes for long, restless, cold nights. A good bag makes for a good night's rest—much needed on an elk hunt!

Today, Colorado is home to nearly 300,000 elk.

Jay's Tip

The key to a comfortable night's sleep in a mummy bag is learning how to turn over: you must turn the entire bag with you. For years I used to try turning inside my mummy bag before I switched to a conventional bag; the knots I would get myself tied up in would drive me nuts, not to mention keep me awake!

Sleeping bags come filled with a variety of insulations, each of which has its advantages and disadvantages. Early designs were filled with duck or goose down and most of the major manufacturers of bags still include down bags in their product line. While down is an excellent insulator, it does have one major drawback. When it gets damp, the loft collapses and the insulation factor decreases significantly—like to absolutely zero.

Today most quality bags are packed with a synthetic fill such as DuPont Hollofil 808, Slumberloft HQ, Polarguard, or DuPont's Thermolite. The difference between these materials is the weight and volume required to achieve a given level of insulation. My bag is a Slumberjack Big Timber 0°F (-18°C) bag filled with Slumberloft HQ. It weighs in at just over five pounds (2.3 kg) and handles most people up to 6 feet-5 inches (195.5 cm).

Ground Pad

The best sleeping bag on the planet will not keep you comfortable for a week at elk camp if it rests on hard, cold ground. A good ground pad or cot makes all the difference. Why not an air mattress, you may ask?

A well-organized cook tent can be a large reason to return year after year.

First, while an air mattress will keep you off the ground, the temperature of the air in the mattress approximates that of the ground it is resting on. Second, years of observation and experience have shown me that most air mattresses lose their air over time. I cannot count the number of times that I have seen hunters awaken to flat or nearly flat air mattresses.

If you just must have an air mattress, consider one of the self-inflating models. These pads are made of open-cell foam encased in an airtight covering. They are popular because they provide the insulation of an open-cell foam pad, are reasonably compact when deflated and offer much of the comfort of an air mattress without having to be blown up. They are, however, quite a bit heavier than closed-cell pads. When you're ready to set up camp, simply open the valve on your sleeping pad and it automatically inflates.

A better bet if you prefer to go light while sleeping near the ground is a combination open-cell/closed-cell foam pad. These pads feature a thin layer of closed-cell (dense) foam that provides a first-rate layer of insulation from the ground, combined with a thicker layer of open-cell foam for comfort. These types of pads are

relatively inexpensive given the amount of comfort they provide. The cost ranges from about $30 to $70 depending on the actual features.

The Cot Option

For years I have slept on a cot covered with a section of egg crate foam that I got free from a local hospital. The advantage to this arrangement is that I can store all of my hunting gear beneath the cot. This serves two purposes: One, the gear serves as additional insulation between the ground and my cot. And two, it keeps all of my stuff safe and out of everyone's way.

I also have one of those cot caddies that straps onto the side of the cot with lots of little pockets to hold stuff like glasses, a small book, a roll of toilet paper and even my rifle if need be.

Finally, don't forget to bring your pillow from home. Sure, some hunters like to show how tough they are by using a knapsack or some other rolled-up piece of gear for a pillow, but honestly, nothing will help you get a great night's rest better than the pillow you sleep with every night. After all, we are talking about creating the ultimate elk camp, right?

COOKING GEAR

Over the years our camp's supply of cooking gear has been amassed from castoffs from the kitchens of our camp members. Rather than describe every item in the camp kitchen, I will hit a few items that I believe can make the difference between a workable camp kitchen and a great camp kitchen.

Our box of flatware looks like a hodgepodge of garage sale rejects. If one could find a single place setting that matches, I would be surprised. What does matter, however, is that we do not use plastic flatware. Although disposable plastic is nice and does not require washing, when it comes to cutting or holding on to a good piece of meat, nothing beats a metal knife and fork.

Coffee is as essential a part of elk camp as a good tent or a well-placed (downwind) latrine. Without it, life just isn't as sweet. Over the years, I have found that there is no substitute for a large stainless steel coffee pot. Ours is a 32-cup (7.7 liter) percolating version. While that may seem like a lot of coffee, it doesn't take long for three or four guys to go through a pot, especially if they love their morning coffee like I do. If you are like me, you preload the coffee pot with water and coffee the night before so all you have to do in the cold, dark predawn hours is fire up the stove and put the pot on. How many times have you done this only to wake up and find the water in the pot that you left outside frozen solid, thereby turning the coffee-making process into a half hour or more nightmare? Avoid this problem by taking the preloaded coffee pot into the sleeping tent with you at night. Usually the radiant heat in the tent is enough to keep the water from freezing.

A ready source of hot water has many, many uses in elk camp.

COFFEE-MAKING TIP

A few years ago, I loaned my coffee pot and tent to some friends for their camp. When their hunt was over, everything came back as expected except the "innards" for my coffee pot— the percolator stem and coffee grounds cup. For two years that coffee pot sat on the shelf of my garage since I couldn't find a source to purchase just the missing parts. I was sharing this problem with my friend one day, and he gave me the perfect solution to my dilemma, one so obvious that I kicked myself for not thinking of it on my own. All I had to do was buy commercial coffee in those sealed filter pouches. Toss one or two into a pot of boiling water and wait. After all, a percolator brews coffee by cycling boiling water through the grounds in the upper container. The only missing feature is that you cannot see the color of the coffee through the little view glass on the top of the pot. So when you think it is ready, just pour a bit of coffee into a cup to see if it looks like you want it to. After a few pots, you'll know how long it takes to brew to the strength you like. An added advantage of this solution is that none of the grounds end up in the bottom of the pot for the last cup (cowboy coffee), and cleaning the pot is as easy as tossing the used coffee pack in the trash. Simple, huh?

Another essential for a great elk camp is a large wash pot. There is nothing more frustrating than to try washing up dishes after a meal in some dinky bowl or, worse yet, by having no washbowl at all and trying the "pour the soap over the pan" approach. For a few bucks you can buy a large canning pot at most surplus stores. These can hold as much as 3 gallons (11 liters) of water and make easy work of cleaning up. In our camp, we dedicate one burner of our four-burner propane stove for keeping hot wash water going. That way, when it's time to clean up, you don't have to wait half an hour for the water to get hot enough to clean the gunk off of your dishes.

Propane Cookstoves

For years I wrestled with those tiny two-burner white-gas stoves for camp cooking. Filling the tank with gas through a tiny funnel (when I remembered to bring it along), then pumping that plunger until my hand and fingers were numb to pressurize the fuel tank. When the propane versions of these came along, I gave up the hassle of white gas and pumping that silly plunger forever.

However, it wasn't until I took my first trip into elk country with an outfitter that I learned how the pros do it. They don't fool around playing musical chairs with the small burners on the fold-up stoves; they bring in the heavy equipment—steel propane cookstoves with as many as four high-output burners. The heavy-duty steel construction assures years of reliability through even the most frequent use. Many of these come from the factory with built-in collapsible legs that, when unfolded and secured, place the cooktop at a comfortable height for most camp chefs. The burners are placed far enough apart to accommodate large fry pans or pots.

Another advantage of these heavy-duty stoves is that the burners can produce as much as 60,000 BTUs of heat for cooking. When hunters start coming back to camp after a long, hard day chasing elk, the last thing they want to deal with is a finicky stove that takes forever to heat a pot of coffee or grill up some chops. Prices can start at around $60 for a basic two-burner version and can run as high as $350 for a deluxe four-burner stove. My three-burner Powder River stove includes an extra-large elongated burner designed to evenly heat a huge stainless steel griddle that is included and is great for frying eggs, bacon or cooking up a batch of pancakes, and it has served our camp and those of many of our friends for over ten years without fail. A good reliable campstove is a must for every first-class elk camp.

WATER PURIFICATION

Depending upon where your camp is, you may or may not have potable drinking water close at hand. If you can truck in your water, great! But if you must use water from a stream or spring for drinking and washing, maintaining a pure supply is often quite time consuming and, frankly, hard work if you have to hand-pump it through a small water purification system. If you do have to purify your own water, a great solution is Katadyn's Base Camp Microfilter.

This system incorporates a reservoir with a built-in filter that can purify 2.6 gallons (9.8 liters) of water in a matter of minutes. The gravity filter is advertised to remove bacteria, giardia and cryptosporidium to EPA standards, and has an activated-carbon core that keeps water tasting and smelling fresh. It filters up to 200 gallons (757 liters) at a rate of 16 ounces (453 g) per minute before cartridge replacement. This system costs around $60.

A portable water purification system provides a safe source of drinking water. It can be used on virtually any size source, even directly from a spring.

Another great way to maintain a clean and pure water supply is a Bota Bottle. While this is the trade name for the product I use, there are a number of vendors that make the same thing. This is a simple pull-up-top water bottle with a filter incorporated in the upper part of the bottle. The filter is the same as that found in most water purification systems. All you have to do is open the bottle, remove the filter, fill it from a running water supply, replace the filter and screw that cap back on. Voila! You have a clean and pure water supply.

If your camp is a bit of a haul from the water supply, you might try what my good friend Danny Farris and his partner JD did on a backcountry bowhunt in Colorado. Their spike camp was a bit of a hike from the creek, so rather than run down to the water every time their small bottles ran dry, Danny emptied the contents of his backpack and lined it with a contractor-grade black plastic trash bag, which he and JD hauled to the creek. They then filled the trash bag with a good supply of water from the stream for the next few days and dropped in some iodine tablets for purification. Ah . . . necessity, the mother of invention.

Comfort at elk camp is nice.

Too much comfort may adversely affect how much time the hunter actually spends in the field!

THE "JOHN"

I realize that for a few this subject may be somewhat of a personal discussion, but for most of us the topic almost borders on the holy. A must for any self-respecting elk camp is a well-designed, well-stocked latrine, better known in elk country as "the pooper."

The basics of such include a sturdy seating arrangement (that has nothing to do with straddling a fallen log), privacy, cover (nobody likes going in the rain or snow), a means to keep things sanitary, and a method of keeping plenty of dry paper handy. If you want the deluxe version, you can toss in a small propane heater and some hunting magazines. However, I strongly advise against this, as such comforts encourage users to spend more time in the pooper than is required, especially if it's really early, really cold, and there is a line of hunters waiting their turn!

If you are looking for a ready-made solution, there are a number of retail options available. One of the best I've seen was in our 2004 camp, the Royal Throne produced by Davis Tent and Awning in Denver, Colorado. It is a complete package, including a handy 3-foot-6-inch by 3-foot-6-inch tent (1 by 1 m) that sets up in minutes, poles, carrying case, and a toilet lid that snaps to a five-gallon bucket. This handy package is available for about $135.

If you are more of the do-it-yourself type, here are a few tips that will make your stay in elk camp a bit more comfortable. You will need:

- 8 × 20-foot (2.4 by 6 m) ripstop tarp with grommets for the walls
- 8 × 8-foot (2.4 by 2.4 m) tarp with grommets for the roof
- 50 feet (15 m) of rope or strong cord
- a few used 1-pound (0.45 kg) coffee cans with lids
- 3 to 5 pounds (1.4 to 2.3 kg) of commercial lime
- a portable toilet seat and stand
- a small collapsible hand shovel
- 5 pounds (2.3 kg) of lime

Collecting these items entails a bit of work but once done, this gear will serve you for years to come.

When you get to elk camp, find a location for your privy downwind of camp, preferably in a stand of timber that allows easy access even in the dark. Often there is one hunter in camp who uses the facility much more than most. This person is highly motivated and usually more than willing to volunteer to build the facility.

Next, locate three small- to medium-size trees that form a triangle with sides of approximately 6 feet (1.8 m) each. If the trunks are not already clear of small limbs up to about 8 feet (2.4 m), you may have to remove a few small branches.

Next dig a hole 1 foot (0.3 m) in diameter and about 4 feet (1.2 m) deep (this depends on how many hunters are in camp and how long you stay, 1 foot/0.3 m per day is a fair rule of thumb) right in the center of the triangle. If you have one, a posthole digger makes this job much easier. Once the hole is complete, wrap the triangle of trees with the larger tarp using the top grommets and rope to attach it to the trees. When you get back to the first tree, simply tie the end of the tarp off at the top, creating a nice entryway.

Use the smaller tarp to construct a simple roof. Once you have enclosed the privy, use the small shovel to put a small amount of lime into the hole for starters. The lime accelerates the process of breaking down the waste and paper and also helps control the odor. Now set your handy-dandy seat over the hole, put a roll of paper in each coffee can and snap the lid in place to keep the paper dry and you're ready to rock and roll.

Chapter 6

A COUPLE GREAT STORIES!

I'll say it again: Elk hunters need to push themselves beyond the fundamentals and learn as much as they can about elk and the environment in which they live. They must also accept total responsibility for their own success and welfare while in the field.

Throughout the year I talk with literally thousands of elk hunters and wanna-be elk hunters. Many of these inquisitive folks ask me the same question over and over again, What are my chances of success? To which I ask, Well, how good of a hunter are you? What do you know about elk and elk hunting?

Often I get responses that redirect my very pointed question in any direction other than at themselves, such as their guide, their fellow hunters, unexpected circumstances, and on and on. My point here is that the hunter who is not willing to accept 100% of the responsibility for the hunt is setting himself or herself up for failure, or worse.

These fundamentals were brought home to me during a recent elk hunt, in the form of painfully acquired yet valuable lessons that I will not soon forget.

RODEO IN THE ROCKIES

Colorado's second combined rifle season in mid-October can be a challenging time to hunt elk for even the most experienced of hunters. The rut is usually over; an army of bowhunters, smoke-pole shooters and riflemen has assaulted the backcountry and pressured the elk from every direction imaginable since the end of August; and the really heavy snows common in later hunting seasons have yet to arrive to drive the elk out of their hideouts in the high country. I have been hunting elk for many years and truth be told, the 2004 season was as tough a hunt as I have ever experienced.

Our gaggle of six hunters, beset with years of anticipation, arrived at base camp alongside our guides and the camp cook about mid-afternoon on Sunday aboard a drained pack-string of horses and mules. We were rather trail weary after almost four hours in the saddle. Though we were sore of seat, we quickly unloaded the gear from the horses and immediately headed for the black timber just beyond camp to begin our search for those elusive branch-antlered beasts.

Four of the first five days of hunting met us with cooler temperatures, accompanied by ground-hugging jet-stream-like winds often blowing rain, sleet, snow or a mixture of all three—sideways for much of the time. I remember sitting on the edge of a meadow surrounded by naked aspens one afternoon, hunkered down as low as I could get and listening to the never-ending wail of the wind just over my head. A 360-class bull could have walked up right behind me and I would not have heard him. Clearly the elk didn't care for the weather any more than we did, because in four days of very hard hunting, my hunting partner, guide and I only managed to eyeball a young spike bull and a couple of cows between us. When the weather turns sour, the elk dig in, far back in the black timber, and usually just wait it out.

Elk are primarily nocturnal feeders.

Day after day our hope had been that the storms, lined up one behind the other, would abate, and we would catch the elk as they exited their hideaways in search of food and water. Unfortunately, Mother Nature had other ideas. But hey, that's elk hunting. It's what we as elk hunters sign on for, right?

Late in the afternoon on our fifth day of trying to pry elk out of the quakie patches and black timber, "Murphy" (of Murphy's Law) reared his head in the form of a single 20-pound (9 kg) "horse-eating" porcupine that took it upon itself to single-handedly "assault" the horse version of the story—three 1,500-pound (680 kg) horses and as many fully armed hunters. Can you visualize this? Three huge men armed to the teeth, atop three massive horses strung out in a line going up the trail to the top of a ridge, when out strolls this little black prickly demon, more or less minding his own business. Actually, I never saw the thorny little devil, but its mere presence in close proximity to our guide's lead horse, as innocent as it may have been, began a shattering chain of events that has forever changed my life.

Have you ever watched a movie where the filmmaker uses slow motion to let the viewer see certain details that might go unnoticed at normal speed? Let me tell you, it really happens. While some of the details are still a bit fuzzy, I can still see the lead horse (in slow motion) come to a decision that all was not well in her world, and that she would rather begin her exit of the county on two legs (the rear ones) rather than the conventional four.

In the space of just a few seconds, all three horses, one after the other like a cascading set of dominoes, had gone absolutely stark raving nuts and departed the area for parts unknown, depositing all three of their riders on the ground in various states of disrepair. Angel, the lead horse, had let her rider, our guide, almost dismount before making a beeline down the mountain while our guide was still trying to get his foot out of the stirrup, flipping him like a cheap burger in the process.

Horse number two began his escape by charging through a grove of aspens. Most of the trees were barely far enough apart for the horse to get through, much less a horse with a large novice rider hanging onto his back for dear life. It looked just like it does on Pro Rodeo on TV.

Not wanting to be left out of all the excitement, my mount, Conway, which in all fairness had been a

real gentleman for five days, opted to avoid whatever was going on up the trail and, like horse number one, initiated his immediate bail-out on two legs rather than four.

If you've never seen the view from the back of a horse whose feet are in the air over your head while pirouetting on his back legs, count yourself blessed. As my steed completed his 180-degree turn, he threw his head violently to one side, snatching the reins from my hands and leaving me with absolutely no control over where he was going. When his front legs were finally reunited with Mother Earth, all he and I could see were the other two horses going down the mountain as if they were snakebit.

Not wishing to try to hang on to a runaway horse going hell-bent for the lead in a three-horse race down the mountain with no reins, I decided to bail out while I still had a vote. At least I think it was my decision, but perhaps not. That part is also still a little fuzzy. Either way I ended up hitting the ground on my right side like a sack of cheap bricks. I lay still for about a minute, making sure I was still alive. A brief examination confirmed my fears that most of my body parts were still working, but a few were not working at all.

When the fog in my head began to clear, I could see Joe, my hunting partner from Dutch Harbor, Alaska, about 100 yards (91 m) down the mountain trying to stand up, then fall down for a while, and then finally stagger to something remotely resembling vertical again.

Once Randy, our guide, was able to stand, he staggered toward me and asked if I was okay. With all the clarity of a coastal-morning fog bank, I told him that I was alive at least but that my right arm wasn't working at all. Assuming I would be okay for a few minutes, he walked down the hill to see what kind of shape Joe was in.

I guess he was satisfied that we were both alright for the time being, so he set off looking for the horses. For what seemed like hours, that was the last either Joe or I saw of another human being.

Like so many other hunters, I grew up reading *Outdoor Life* magazine. As a youngster in the South, I was fascinated by tales of massive grizzlies roaming the wilds of Wyoming and the majestic elk and mule deer that lived high in the Rockies. Having been no farther west than Arkansas until I was almost a teenager, all such creatures and stories were but visions in my dreams.

Early morning and late afternoon are prime times for elk hunting.

There was, however, one section of every issue that I always turned to first. *This Happened to Me* was a cartoon-type feature that reenacted some disastrous event that had befallen some unfortunate outdoorsman. Whether it was an unwitting hunter stumbling upon a sow grizzly with cubs or an errant fisherman who had fallen through the ice, most stories were cases of catastrophe and survival, events where a person had to really rely upon skill, wits and knowledge of the outdoors to come out alive.

I think what attracted me to these articles the most was the fact that the proverbial "Me" could have been anyone, even myself! It brought the story and the message home to a very personal level. In every story the author managed to embed some realized truth from the event. The objective was to pass on a lesson learned in the hope that others would gain from the presented misfortune.

Such was my story. While the triggering event may have been somewhat calamitous, and was surely an accident, the real gems are the lessons that were learned or reinforced along the way.

Lesson Learned #1:
Murphy Is Alive and Well

The first of Murphy's Laws states, "If anything can go wrong, it will." Murphy's second law states that, "If there is a possibility of several things going wrong, the one that causes the most damage (and busts your chops) will be the one to go wrong."

As a former United States Air Force aviator, I spent a considerable part of my training planning for the unexpected. From day one in flight school we learned that every time we climbed into the cockpit, this invisible Murphy guy would climb in with us and go along for the ride. As a result, in all those years and thousands of hours in the cockpit, I never took a flight where I failed to prepare myself for the possibility of something going wrong. More so, even though I was a crew member of a two-seat jet fighter, I never assumed that the other guy in the plane would be there to deal with whatever problem arose. I knew that if I had my stuff together and knew what procedures to follow— what courses of action were necessary—I would be doing all I could to maximize my chances for survival, as well as that of my fellow crew member and the aircraft. I never depended on the other guy to do it for me.

Lesson Learned #2:
Look Out for Yourself

Elk hunting is fraught with all manner of potential risks, including surprise storms, physical injury, or even becoming disoriented in an immense and unforgiving land. Research indicates that few hunters give such risks any significant thought; even fewer consider what they would do if something dire happened. Such thoughts are usually placed far back in the mind, frequently under the category of "I'll deal with that later, if and when it ever happens," or "that only happens to other hunters." Plans are not in place, and contingencies for the unexpected are often not discussed with fellow hunters or family. In essence, when we fail to plan for the unforeseen, we are in fact planning to fail and setting the stage for some future disaster. I was very fortunate in that my injuries—a severely dislocated shoulder, a torn rotator cuff and a piece of bone torn away from my shoulder—were relatively minor compared to what could have happened. Well, let's get back to the story.

After Joe and I had gathered our wits, we began to analyze the situation we were faced with. Almost immediately my Air Force survival training kicked in and I determined that we needed to come up with a course of action and we needed it quick. From the sun's low position on the horizon, I could tell that it would be getting dark (and much colder) soon. Both Joe and I had suffered what we suspected were severe injuries, leaving us in acute pain and somewhat debilitated. Joe was telling me that every time he took a breath, his ribs shot fiery bolts throughout his body, making it difficult for him to breathe and walk. My shoulder was so damaged that it racked me with some of the most intense pain I had ever known, making focusing on anything, much less a survival plan, that much more difficult.

I am rarely without my GPS, a part of my essential kit of "elk hunting stuff." However, on this particular day, I had hastily decided to leave my GPS back at camp, since I knew that our trusty guide relied on his GPS and always had it in his daypack. Wrong—bad decision! Never, ever leave camp without your GPS! In my desire to lighten my daypack, I had broken one of my longtime personal rules by relying on someone else for my own welfare while hunting.

Navigating stands of dead timber is just one of the challenges of hunting elk country.

With the sun getting lower by the minute, I knew that we had to get back to camp for help. Fortunately, over the course of five days of hunting, I had become acquainted with a few prominent landmarks. I also knew in general terms where our camp was in relationship to these.

By visualizing our current position in relationship to these three landmarks, Joe and I were able to figure out the general direction we would have to travel to get back to camp. Unfortunately, there was one problem: neither of us was in any shape to handle the valleys and hills that lay along a straight-line path back to camp. Joe and I decided that if we were to make it back to camp, we would have to keep to higher ground. This meant traveling a much longer and more roundabout route.

So off we went. Two banged-up hunters looking like something out of a rodeo wreck hobbling up a game trail at a pace that would make a snail look like a NASCAR racer. I really have to give my hunting partner and friend Joe the lion's share of the credit. With a useless arm dangling toward the ground like a broken wing and having to walk like Quasimodo to minimize the pain, I couldn't possibly carry my backpack and its internal water supply. So Joe, fiery dinged-up ribs and all, was the hero and volunteered to carry both of our packs. Thinking that going into shock was a possibility for each of us, we stopped regularly for water and to check up on each other for any signs of shock or dehydration.

Jay's Tip

Never head out into the backcountry alone, especially in big country like the Colorado Rockies.

After what seemed like three or four hours, but was in reality possibly just an hour or so, we saw our guide and one of the other camp guides riding toward us on the game trail with our wayward horses in tow.

Two memories of this scene remain vividly etched in my mind. First, not seeing anything resembling remorse on the face of my horse, I really wanted to go over to him and give him a piece of my mind . . . or a bit more. Remember the scene in front of the saloon with Mongo and the horse in the movie *Blazing Saddles?* Second, I recall looking up at my horse and thinking to myself, *No way.*

So, in as cordial a way as I could think of, I promptly informed the young guide that there was no possible way for me to climb up on the horse with a busted-up arm. More so, with my recent rodeo experience as fresh in my mind as an NFL Monday night replay, there was no way I was going to climb back up on any horse in the foreseeable future. I even recall that for a brief second, the image of a heavyweight boxing champ hovering over his fallen opponent flashed through my mind, with his ominous words of warning echoing, "If you know what's good for you, you'll stay down too!"

Believing that my injuries would require professional medical attention as soon as possible, and thinking that Joe might be in the same shape or worse, I suggested that the guide hustle back to camp and get on the cell phone to the Search and Rescue folks and get a helicopter in the air. In response the young guide informed me, "You've probably just got a dislocated shoulder. I think I can probably fix that!" With all the willpower within me, I just thanked him for his offer and requested the helicopter again.

Lesson Learned #3: Sound Judgment Rules

So Joe and I bowed our heads into the wind and once again stepped off on our trek up the ridge and toward camp. Having to keep to the higher ground to avoid any significant climbing that neither of us could handle, our route took us on a fairly roundabout path back to camp, taking the better part of another hour.

When we finally reached camp, word of our misfortune had already gotten around. The camp cook, to her credit, had already placed the call that I requested to the outfitter's trailhead camp, which placed a follow-up call to the county sheriff's office to initiate the rescue operation. I walked into camp on my own and made my way into our tent, where I tried to make myself as comfortable and stable as possible.

By now my entire body was shaking uncontrollably. Whether this was from the adrenaline, the shock, the cool outside temperature or a combination of all three, I don't recall. I do remember that my biggest fears the entire time, and those that consumed most of my thoughts, were how to keep from going into shock and how I was going to break this news to my new wife.

I am blessed with the most wonderful wife a guy could ever ask for. She loves me with all of her heart and encourages me daily to pursue my other loves, elk hunting and writing about elk hunting. However, years ago as a teenager, Rae Ann had lost her best friend in a horseback riding accident. Now after only a few months of marriage, this happens to me. I had to find a way to let her know about the accident while assuring her that I was in good hands and would be fine. I sent a message via the camp cook to the outfitter to hold off calling Rae Ann until I was onboard the helicopter and in the hands of medical professionals, thinking that would minimize her fears. Boy, do I have a lot to learn. Wives are going to worry regardless. It is their nature.

It is important to note that I have no medical training beyond some basic level Red Cross and Air Force survival school first-aid courses. About all I knew of traumatic injury was that in many cases shock was a possibility, could be deadly and should always be treated accordingly. Since then, I've learned that shock is usually caused by an abrupt loss of blood, which was not the case here. Nevertheless, I encourage anyone who plans to spend time in the backcountry to take a comprehensive course in first aid, so that if and when the time comes, you will have knowledge and skills necessary to render appropriate care. This is definitely an area where it's wise to go beyond the fundamentals. Your life or that of someone you care about may depend on it.

Lesson Learned #4:
Never Leave an Injured Person Alone

Time seemed to drag on forever as I lay there alone, anticipating the sound of the rescue helicopter. There was virtually no position that I could assume that would relieve the nerve-racking pain, which by now—since the adrenaline had worn off—was almost debilitating.

That's right, I was alone.

I guess everyone got so caught up in preparing for the helicopter that they forgot they had an injured party in camp. When one of the other hunters finally came into the tent, I asked him if he would mind checking on me from time to time. From that moment on, one of my fellow hunters was always there by my side. What a great bunch of guys. I owe every one of them a huge debt of gratitude.

Lesson Learned #5:
Prayer Is Always Welcome

I had been lying there for about an hour when one of the other hunters I really didn't know, Spencer Ruff, walked in and asked how I was doing. I told him I was doing as well as possible given the circumstances, at which point he sat down on my cot and asked if he could pray for me. I am no stranger to prayer, but this was new, and even now I am overcome with emotion as I relive the moment, remembering the generosity, sensitivity and Christian brotherly love of my newfound friend as he bowed his head and prayed for me.

Just as the sun began to settle behind the purple mountains—they really are purple when the sun is just right—to the west, I heard the most welcomed sound I had heard all week: that of rotors tearing through the cold mountain air. I knew then that my ordeal was almost over and that I would be fine.

With hunter-orange vests volunteered from every hunter and guide in camp forming a makeshift emergency landing zone, a Flight for Life helicopter carrying angels of mercy landed just a few hundred yards (m) from my tent.

In no time a flight nurse and medical technician were beside me checking my vitals and preparing me for the quickest trip out of the mountains I have ever had. In minutes we were airborne and on our way to an outstanding team of professionals at Saint Mary's Hospital Emergency Room in Grand Junction, Colorado.

Post-Hunt Update

Unknown to me or anyone else in camp at the time, including Joe, the result of Joe's encounter was far more damaging than anyone knew—three broken ribs. Joe is as tough a guy as I have ever met, and no one hunts harder or longer than Joe did on our trip. Earlier I referred to Joe as a hero and that is exactly what he is, though he will likely argue the point when he reads this.

Busted ribs and all, Joe hauled both sets of our gear all those miles (km) back to camp without a single complaint! I pray that I am never again in such circumstances, but should I be, I hope I am fortunate enough to be hunting with Joe Novosel or a man like this true American hero. God bless you, Joe. I will never forget you. Thank you!

Sharing stories over a hot cup of coffee at day's end with a hunting buddy is a cherished part of elk hunting.

TWO MONSTER BULLS, TWO MEMORIES

Four of us were dead tired and just crashed in a blowdown midway down the slope of one of the steepest and most treacherous mountainsides I had ever hunted. My hunting partners for the week, TJ Shiimunek, host of Gammy Creek Outdoors TV, his videographer Pat Walderzak, guide Brian Parks, and I were surrounded by an impenetrable forest of ancient western red cedars, many towering well beyond the 100-foot (30 m) mark, and alders so thick that horizontal visibility was often limited to 10 feet (3 m) or less.

Our small band of hunters was recuperating after spending four exhausting hours with our noses to the ground tracking the blood trail of a monster bull that had been arrowed two days earlier on the other side of the mountain by TJ's business partner, Zach Poff. To say we were all tired would have been nothing short of gross sarcasm. One look at our motley crew with our bows and gear scattered about the forest floor would not have led one to believe that we were in pursuit of anything more than a good nap.

An Up-Close Encounter

Each of us had come to Idaho in September with dreams of arrowing a 300-class or better Pope and Young bull. However, monster bulls were the furthest things from our minds during these few moments of respite.

As I half dozed with my back up against a fallen cedar, out of the corner of my eye I noticed Pat sit up and reach for his camera while slowly turning his head in my direction. To my amazement his eyes were as wide as saucers, and all he could manage to whisper were three brief words that would trigger the beginning of an elk-country encounter that I will treasure for the rest of my life, those words were "bull . . . big bull." And then, all you-know-what broke loose.

Sixteen years of pursuing these majestic antlered beasts throughout my home state of Colorado, mostly as a rifle hunter, could never have prepared me for what would happen next and how fast it would all come together.

If a bull comes in silently, you must be prepared for the shot with little warning.

Like being frozen in time, a bull pays attention to the slightest disturbance.

For those of you who have experienced such an up close encounter, you probably empathize with me as I recall some of the many thoughts that passed through my brain in a matter of seconds: Don't move too quickly; move your eyes first, not your head; identify the clear shooting lanes. Where is the wind? Are there cows close by that can bust me? Where will the bull appear? Make sure that the angle to the target is good; don't look at the rack; focus on a small 2-inch (5 cm) spot behind the shoulder. Don't look at the rack, fool! What's the range to the primary shooting lane? 20 yards (18 m)? What's the range to the back-up lane? 25 yards (23 m)? Which is the correct pin? The green one? No, the yellow one. No, the green 20-yard (18-m) one with a little adjustment? Yep. Does the vertical angle to the target require a range adjustment? Nope, not enough to worry about. Check the wind again; don't look at the rack. And on it went….

Breathe calmly; think back position; shoulder position; wrist. Breathe again. Finger behind the trigger of the release; draw; anchor; now, finger around the trigger. Don't punch it; take your time; clear the target area. Okay, now don't breathe; focus; take your time. Where are the shakes? There are supposed to be shakes. Just a little back pressure for the shot. Focus on the small spot….

As the shooter with the honors, I ever so slowly reached for my PSE Vengeance bow that was leaning against a fallen log just an arm's length away, while moving my eyes in the direction where all the commotion was coming from. For those interested, I was packing Easton Axis ST 400s and NAP 100-grain Nitron broadheads.

As I strained to see through the dense undergrowth, a thunderous bawl that made the hair on the back of my neck stand straight up erupted just 40 yards (37 m) from our hideaway. Within seconds the ivory-tipped rack of a monster bull that was more than wide enough to bracket the top of a VW bug began to magically appear a few inches (cm) at a time, coming up the side of the bench where we were hiding in the dense cedar and alders. Having just snatched two cows from an even larger bull that we had named the Growler, far down the mountain, this bruiser was really full of himself, screaming as he shredded limbs from a 3-inch (7.6 cm) cedar two at a time. To say the least, there was no shortage of testosterone and this big boy was really worked up. Thus, after three days of some of the toughest, sometimes near vertical, high-country hunting I had ever experienced, all of my instincts, knowledge, skill and practice came online and kicked into high gear telling me that it was time to get down to business.

A Hunt with High Expectations

My first Idaho bowhunt had its beginnings four months earlier, when I was contacted by a friend about helping him book elk, mule deer and bear hunters for his outfit. He told me that one of his permitted areas held some very nice bulls and that he wanted my help to book some additional hunters.

Having developed a reputation as a reliable elk-hunting consultant over the past twelve years, I don't recommend the services of new outfitters or landowners until after I've hunted with them personally. Experience has taught me that any outfit can sound good, but the true measurement of the quality and integrity of an outfitting business can only be made by spending time in elk camp hunting with them.

I shared this philosophy with my friend and all he said was, "When do you want to come out and hunt?" That year, my hunting season was already pretty full with a Colorado rifle elk hunt in mid-October and an Ohio bowhunt for whitetail in late October to early November, but the opportunity to get what I hoped would be a 300-class or better bull with a bow was just too much to pass up. I made a few calls and called my friend back to tell him that I would arrive on September 14.

Due to the extreme amount of hunting pressure on public land in my home state of Colorado, I usually counsel my hunting clients to seriously consider taking the first legal animal that they have a good shot at.

However, since the outfitter had told me that his area had more than its share of 300-class or better bulls, I set my standards for this hunt a bit higher. Come what may, it would be a 300-plus-class bull or nothing for me on this particular hunt.

I have always believed that if you want to hunt really fired-up bulls during the rut, the last two weeks of September are often your best bet. Accordingly, I was not surprised when the rut in the area around our camp started to gain momentum on September 15, our first day out, and then kicked into high gear two days later with bulls bugling all over the range that we were hunting.

"The Growler."

Waiting for a bull to turn and give you a good shot can be nerve wracking.

Mid-morning on the second day found one of my hunting partners, Zach Poff, and his videographer, Ryan Themm, about 900 feet (274 m) up a steep brush-covered slope above a bowl that was known to hold a heavily beamed 6 × 6 bull. The word from our guides was that each morning the bull would climb out of the hole where he spent the night using a known route to cross the higher ridge above the bowl through a saddle. Zach and Ryan had left camp far before daybreak with a plan to waylay this bruiser as he made his way toward his bedding area on the opposite side of the saddle.

As it so often happens, elk fail to read our playbook and come up with some pretty surprising plays of their own. Expecting the big bull to be coming up the slope from the bowl below, Zach and Ryan set up accordingly, with Ryan playing the role of both videographer and caller. Ryan began by making a few brief, high-pitched bugles imitating an immature bull, followed by a series of estrus cow calls, a strategy frequently used to rile up a more mature bull by making him think that there is a young bull nearby with a few cows tagging along. Almost immediately a bull responded to Ryan's calls, not from down the ridge as expected, but from up the mountain. Score so far, Elk 1, Hunters 0.

According to Zach and Ryan, this bad boy was madder than a thousand hornets at the thought of another bull having snuck into his territory, and he was determined to let someone know just how ticked off he was. Zach and Ryan decided to quickly swap positions so that Ryan would be calling from behind Zach, who was now the uphill member of the team. No sooner had they swapped positions than the bull appeared, working his way through the alders with fire in his eyes, looking to pick a fight with the intruder bull that he had just heard. Now the pace was picking up. So as not to be detected, Zach drew his bow when the bull was looking away and then he knelt below a small alder bush. Zach must have felt like he was at full draw forever, but in reality it was only a few seconds before the bull was on him.

The monster bull had come in quickly and stopped a mere 5 feet (1.5 m) from where Zach was hidden at full draw beneath the alders, directly under the bull's neck and chest. I wish I could say that with my 40 years of big game hunting experience I would have been as cool and collected as 25-year-old Zach was, but I seriously doubt I would have had half the control

that this younger hunter showed under such extreme circumstances. Way to go Zach! Had it been me, there might have been a change of clothes required after such a close encounter.

According to Zach, a number of things were going through his mind as he hid beneath this enormous bull that was all but drooling on his cap, not the least of which was the very real possibility of getting stomped or even gored if the bull discovered him. With no 5-foot (1.5 m) pin on his sight, Zach waited until the bull looked over him for the other elusive bull before placing his entire sight pin guard on the bull's vitals just feet (m) away. Zach later told us that before the shot, he wasn't even sure if the arrow would clear the bow before it hit the bull. But clear the bow it did. Though the shaft didn't have time to achieve maximum velocity, it had plenty of juice to bury itself all the way up to the vanes in the bull's vitals.

Following the shot, the confused bull bolted from sight back into the impenetrable brush as quickly as he had come. Meanwhile, Zach and Ryan collapsed and tried to recover from what would likely be the closest encounter of their lives with the bull of a lifetime.

A Bugler's Tale

At about the same time, my guide Brian and I were on the opposite side of the same mountain. We had scrambled 1 foot (30 cm) at a time about 1,000 feet (305 m) up a killer grade that was near 50 degrees (vertical) in some places. Oftentimes we would have to hold on to alder limbs and literally swing from bush to bush to keep from rolling back down the mountain. To cover the racket that our trek was making, we would make cow calls from time to time, tossing in a bugle for good measure here and there. Brian was packing a Terminator bugle that was so powerful it hurt my ears when he cut loose with it, and since the rut had hardly had time to build up much steam, it wasn't producing much results.

I asked Brian if he would mind if I tried a couple from my smaller Pack Bugle, which imitates a much younger and less mature bull. He said, "You wrote the book; sure, go for it." I laughed and just shook my head, knowing that he was really just having a little fun at my expense. I whipped out the Pack Bugle and did my best to sound like some worked-up but youthful bull looking for love. My first attempt produced the same results as that of Brian's Terminator—nada.

Routinely testing the wind is a bull's natural habit.

Every instinct in me, however, told me that the rut should be on, so why were the bulls being so quiet? I wondered. I waited about two minutes and let go with a second short bugle and before I had finished chuckling, two bulls quickly responded from nearby uphill. These boys were close. Their bugles seemed to surround us, echoing off trees and undergrowth. The dark timber was so thick, it was hard to tell exactly how far away the bulls were. Brian told me that in such thick timber the elk are usually closer than you think, so we estimated that the bull directly uphill was around 60 yards (55 m) out, and the bull at our two o'clock was probably more like 75 yards (69 m) away. Based on the varying volume of his bugles, we determined the uphill bull was probably working back and forth along a game trail that Brian knew of. The other bull was showing less interest, probably because he was a younger bull and didn't want any part of what was going on over our way.

The underbrush was too thick and the slope too steep to try a sneak. So for what seemed like the next half hour, Brian and I tried every call and trick in the book to lure one of these bulls down to us for a shot, but they were not going to have any of it. Since we didn't hear any cows, we assumed that while their testosterone was on the rise, it had not yet hit the point where either bull was ready for a real fight. Though we were not able to close the deal on these bulls, the adventure sure started my blood flowing and I realized that the hunt had only just begun.

Regrouping

With bulls beginning to bugle all around us, as well as the other hunters in camp, we decided to try to hook up with the rest of our group and develop some sort of plan rather than continue to bust brush at random. This can be a real challenge, especially if you're hunting with strangers who do not yet know each other's skills and abilities. The temptation is for each hunter or hunting team to head off in random directions. However, years of experience has taught me that working together with a plan almost always produces better results in the long run. So we headed back to camp to work on a group strategy.

Soon after arriving at camp, Zach and Ryan walked in with the "agony and ecstasy" tale of their close encounter, all of which was caught on videotape. Following the shot, Zach and Ryan had waited for

the bull to lie down. After what they thought was a respectable wait, they set off along a spotty blood trail.

Seeing bubbles in the blood, Zach was sure that his arrow had taken out at least one of the bull's lungs and that he wouldn't be able to go far and must have crashed nearby in the thick brush. After hours of scouring the mountain for Zach's bull to no avail, they decided to return to camp for more help.

Since Ryan had captured the entire event on videotape, we took turns watching the encounter unfold through the camera's small viewfinder. When the tape came to the part with the monster bull almost standing over Zach, looking directly over his head as Zach remained frozen at full draw in the brush, all you could hear was, "You've gotta be kidding me!" Well, that's sort of what they said.

With a wounded bull on the mountain, we agreed to focus on recovering the bull. So for the better part of that afternoon and most of the following morning, teams of hunters, packers and guides combed nearly every inch (cm) of the mountainside where Ryan had taken his shot, but in the end . . . no bull.

In the afternoon following Ryan's encounter, TJ, Pat, my guide Brian and I set off for the top of the mountain in hopes of locating another shooter bull. Upon reaching the summit, we were treated to one of the most spectacular views of the hunt, as we were able to take in hundreds of square miles (km) of mountains and timber. We spent a few extra minutes on the summit taking pictures and then headed off down the mountain in search of Mr. Big.

After about an hour of working our way diagonally across the slope, we decided to set up and glass the draw below us. We knew that a good water source ran down the middle of the draw and hoped that with the protection provided by the steep slopes on both sides and the water, it would hold elk. After glassing for about 10 minutes, I bugled briefly to determine if perhaps anyone was home. Almost immediately the deep raspy bugle of a mature bull answered my bugle from far below. I bugled back. This conversation continued for about half an hour. I could tell by the change in this monster's tone that he was moving back and forth along a line running from us to him. My guess was that he had cows with him and that when he would reach our end of the herd, a satellite bull would try to come in from the other end and cut out some of his cows, so he would charge back the other way.

Early-morning is a great time to hunt.

Sitting on the bluff, we had heard the second bull on and off as we called. Knowing that we would not be able to make it down to the bull with the wind in our favor before dark, we decided to leave and return the next morning, hoping to approach the bull from a different angle and make a close approach with the wind in our favor. As we gathered our gear and got up to leave the area, someone said, "That bull sure does growl at lot." Thus we named this bull the Growler.

A New Plan

That evening we made a plan to have the packers drop us off at the top of the mountain early the next morning. They would then return to camp and take a truck and park it across the river at the base of the mountain. We would hunt down the mountain throughout the next day, crossing the river and taking the truck back to camp that night. Knowing that our departure the next morning would come far too soon, we all ate quickly and called it an early night. With visions of the Growler dancing in all of our heads, needless to say sleep did not come easily for at least one of us—me.

The following morning dawned chilly, with a bit of fog floating in the deep mountain valleys like a downy blanket with holes all over the place and mountaintops poking through. The upper slopes of the mountain were steep, so we elected to wait at the top until it was light enough to see without flashlights to begin moving toward the Growler. As we made our trek down, we began to hear two bulls bugling back and forth, coming from far below, but it was clear that neither of these was the Growler. Both sounded like younger bulls.

Sometimes, however, bugles fool you and you can end up with a mature bull in your lap thinking it is a raghorn coming in. The cedar and alders were thick, so it was difficult to tell how far away these bulls were. Occasionally we would cow call just to keep their attention. On two separate occasions, we thought one or the other of the bulls was coming in and set up, only to have the setup blown by swirling winds each time. The four of us worked the two bulls for about an hour with no luck before moving on down the mountain.

As we were making our way through some underbrush, we came across a blood trail that appeared to be less than 24 hours old. Determining the age of a blood trail can be difficult if there has been rain or moisture in the air that keeps the blood wet. Though we were not certain about age, we set off on the trail anyway. Early on, the trail was fairly clear and consistent and appeared to have come from the top of the mountain along a route that paralleled the one we had taken. We quickly surmised that this might be the trail of Zach's bull, so for the next four hours our gang of scruffy camo-clad warriors put our hunt on hold and took to the trail like a pack of Tennessee bloodhounds.

Knowing that there was good water at the bottom and that wounded animals often try to make their way to a water source, we were fairly certain where this bull was going. It was just a matter of staying with the trail until we caught up with the bull. Many times we would lose the trail in the heavy brush, only to pick it up again. Unfortunately, however, the trail ended in a cedar thicket near a big blood blowout. We couldn't figure out how the bull could have made it past this point with so much loss of blood, but this blood didn't have the frothy look of the blood near where Zach took his shot. This blood was much darker with very little froth. My guess is that Zach's shot missed the near lung and either clipped the far lung or more than likely hit the liver. Either way, this bull had come a long way.

Eventually we all agreed that there was not much hope in finding the bull, so we resumed our hunt for the Growler farther down the mountain. By this time we were all pretty tired from the tracking, so we decided to take a short break and grab a bite to eat in a sunny little blowdown on a small bench, and it was here that my encounter with the broad-beamed bull exploded.

Finally, a Shot

In my years of elk hunting, I have seen quite a few bulls with more mass than this fellow, but none with such an expansive outside spread from antler tip to tip. The main beams of most bulls leave the skull at an upturned angle; this monster's rack turned almost 90 degrees to the left and right before sweeping to the vertical.

As I mentioned earlier, this bull was making his way up the mountain at a pretty good clip with two cows that he had just hijacked from another bull, probably the Growler, down below. The cows were in the lead and I really didn't want to blow this deal and get busted by one of the cows while drawing my bow before the bull stepped into a good shooting lane.

Since I could clearly see the cows moving up the hill, I assumed that they would see me draw so I held off, waiting for them to move on past me and back into the alder brush. All the while a bull of a lifetime is getting closer and closer trying to catch up to his cows.

I picked out what I thought would be the perfect shooting lane for a broadside shot at 20 yards/18 m (no time for a range finder) if the bull cooperated. I came to full draw just before the bull stepped into the lane, but as I was starting to settle the pin behind his shoulder, the bull made an abrupt turn to his left to get around a tree, leaving me with nothing but a tail-on shot, which I wouldn't take.

Immediately I began searching for another clear shooting lane. As the bull was constantly weaving through the thick undergrowth, it was nearly impossible to predict where he would next pop out into the clear.

Still at full draw, I was watching the bull work his way around a couple of cedars, while at the same time trying to mentally range a small opening where I thought he would come into the clear.

Finally, the bull stepped into a small lane but was lower than I anticipated. He must have stepped into a shallow depression. I knew I had only a second to make the decision. I mentally estimated the range to be 25 yards (23 m). Settling the 20-yard (18 m) pin to compensate for the downward angle of the shot just behind the shoulder, I released.

To this day, I can still envision the scene playing out in slow motion, frame by frame. The bull is momentarily frozen with his head turned looking straight at me, trying to make sense of this camo-clad image before him, the black Easton Axis arrow with a white wrap and white vanes is tracking directly toward the bull for a perfect double lung shot. My eyes move to those of the bull. I can without a doubt see something register in his eyes as they grow wider yet still focused on me that all is not right, but he cannot figure it out so he remains steady. Again my eye picks up the white vanes still in flight, closer now but still on track. Then it happens. The arrow disappears. No warning, no nothing. It's there one second and gone the next. My ear detects the whack of a solid hit and the bull whirls and crashes back down the mountain. It's over—no, it's not over.

Now the adrenaline hits. My mind races, how far will he go? How are we going to get him out of this, the most desolate of places? Did Pat get the shot on tape? Now TJ is rushing over with high-fives. Everyone is pumped, especially me. With about a gallon of adrenaline now rushing through my veins like it was shot out of a fire hose, I cannot even manage to hit TJ's hand with a return to his high-five. Air. Where did all the air go? I am caught up in the rush of the event! Thirty seconds ago I was almost asleep, now this.

Then comes the news that none of us expected or wanted to hear. Pat has rewound the videotape and thinks that there may have been a problem with the shot. No, that's not possible. I had seen the arrow mere feet (m) from the bull's vitals still on track. I heard the whack of impact. How could this be? As Pat studies the videotape, TJ walks over to where the bull was standing and discovers the truth.

There, imbedded in a log lay my perfectly clean arrow. A few feet (m) short of where the bull had stood just a few minutes before was the answer to the mystery. The small, nearly invisible yet neatly severed stem that my arrow had inadvertently struck on its way to the bull's vitals.

What a Hunt!

Rags to riches, victory and defeat, life and death, often it seems that mere seconds are all that stand between the two. In this instance, I was unable to close the deal. However, I experienced one of the most remarkable hunts of my life. I now have a memory that I can play back over and over again, reliving every heart-pounding second, anytime I choose. Traveling around the country speaking at shows and hunting events, I tell this story time and again. And every time I get the same response: What an opportunity! What a hunt!

I included this story in this book for two reasons. First, to reinforce that I believe elk hunting is more about the experience than the end result. It is about the challenges of the journey from valley floor to mountaintop. It is about being witness to and participant in a legacy passed down through the generations. Hunting joins us together in one of God's greatest creations—elk country. The second reason I include this tale of the most physically challenging hunt of my life at age fifty-two is to emphasize the importance of becoming "a true hunter." Well . . . I am a hunter, you may say. What is he talking about? I mean that in seventeen years of elk hunting, I have been witness to many "wannabe" hunters whom I can only describe as folks casually taking their rifle or bow for a stroll in the woods, who I am sure are not having the type of hunt they desire. Are these the hunters who regularly have elk back straps for supper, or at least get to experience moments like those in the story just told? In all honesty, probably not.

So what's the difference between those who consistently have opportunities like the one I shared and those who do not? You have to be willing to do whatever it takes, to go the extra mile (km). You must have the knowledge, the confidence, the gear, the skill, the perseverance and the internal drive to make it happen.

You know what, that bruiser bull is still out there, and I hope to return to that Idaho elk country. He and I have another date, and I intend to be there for the dance!

White tips on antlers make them easier to count.

Appendix
CHOOSING A GUIDE

Why should you hire a reputable hunting consultant? Here is the account of a very good personal friend, Tracy Breen, who was duped by an unprincipled individual who called himself an outfitter.

"Oftentimes when Easterners head out West, our heads are dancing with dreams of what we think elk hunting really is. We may have a good idea of what elk are and what hunting them is like, but we don't always know what to expect from an outfitter. This is especially true if you have never had the privilege of hunting with a guide.

"Although I am an experienced hunter, finding a good outfitter can be hard and there are just as many bad outfitters as good. On a 2003 trip to Colorado, I searched for weeks before I made the final decision on an outfitter to hunt with. Why did I choose this guide? He said all the right things. He knew what to tell me to convince me that his was a first-class and reputable outfit, but he was crafty enough not to tell me too much. I was told we would have Class-A accommodations. I was told I would be into elk every day. I was told I would be hunting with experienced guides. I was told I would have a 90 percent chance of getting a shot. I ate this up like a kid in a candy store. Unfortunately, Class-A accommodations turned out to be a pop-up camper with a propane heater, and we never saw an elk. Needless to say, we never got a shot and from my point of view our guides didn't have any experience guiding bowhunters."

Happily, Tracy had the opportunity to return to Colorado for another bowhunt in 2004, and bagged his first bull elk while hunting at the famous Three Forks Ranch. I spoke with ranch manager, Jay Linderman,

some months after Tracy's hunt. Knowing full well the unfortunate experience that Tracy had endured in 2003, Jay told me that his team was determined to do their best to help Tracy achieve his lifetime goal of harvesting a nice bull. On the fifth day of his hunt, Tracy's dream came true when he harvested a very nice 5 × 5 bull. Good job, Tracy!

Hunting consultants are not the solution for everyone. But if you don't live in or near elk country and don't know where to start planning your hunt or whom to trust, consider contacting a reputable hunting consultant. It is their job to help hunters locate exactly the right hunt, while avoiding problems like the one Tracy encountered.

Here are some questions you should ask any guide you are considering:
- How much experience does the guide have?
- What is the guide's success ratio?
- How many hunters will be in the party?
- How much land will be available to hunt—private or public?
- Will horses and pack mules be used?
- Will camp be in the backcountry or at a ranch setting?
- What supplies will be provided and what will I need to bring?
- What former clients can I call for a reference?

Here are just a few Web sites that can help you begin your search for a reputable hunting consultant:
- www.ElkCamp.com
- www.TheOutfitterNetwork.com
- www.biggamehunt.net
- www.huntingoutfitters.com
- www.huntingtop10.com

FIELD DRESSING YOUR ELK

Now the real fun—spelled w.o.r.k.—begins. Okay, so you have somewhere between 500 and 1,000 pounds (227 and 454 kg) of elk lying on the ground at your feet. What do you do?

With the proper tools, you can use one of two popular and time-tested ways to field dress your animal: the conventional method or the gutless method.

While it is not impossible to field dress your elk alone, the task will be much easier if you have a hunting partner to help. A partner also comes in handy for help in stabilizing the animal and when it comes time to bone and pack the rascal back to camp.

Tools & Stuff

Start with a quality, sharp hunting knife (two are better) with strong blades and no-slip handles. This is another one of those times you really don't want to go cheap, as many inexpensive imported knives are made of low-grade steel that doesn't want to hold an edge and can break with only a minor amount of lateral pressure to the blade. Benchmade, Buck, Gerber, Kershaw, SOG, and Spyderco make excellent hunting knives.

You also need a sharpening stone. I carry a folding diamond dust sharpener and a small ceramic V-shaped sharpener for quick jobs. If you need to do some serious knife sharpening, you can't beat a Lansky sharpening system. Mine has three separate hones. They take up a little more room, but when it comes to getting the job done on almost any knife, they are tough to beat.

You will want to have a lightweight saw for removing the skullcap if you decide to take the antlers home without the entire head.

To round out your gear, you need four or five heavy-duty cotton game bags and about 50 feet (15 m) of nylon cord. If you can afford to spend a few extra bucks, you can get ultra-low-stretch cord at many backpacker shops like REI or EMS. This really comes in handy back at camp when it's time to hang up your game to cool and keep away from animals. I've had some of the less expensive cord stretch out during the night due to the weight and find the game bag hanging substantially lower than where I left it the night before. It's your call.

The Conventional Method

Unless someone else volunteers to do the work—not likely—you will have about an hour and a half worth of work preparing your elk for the trip back to camp. Here are the steps I follow:

1. Position the animal with the head uphill and the tail downhill. This helps facilitate draining blood and fluids from the body cavity once you open it up.

2. With a sharp knife, make a deep cut completely around the rectum, being careful not to puncture or cut the intestine. Pull the end of the rectum to make sure that it is separated from the tissues connecting it to the pelvic canal. With a piece of string or a strong rubber band, tie off the end of the rectum to prevent droppings from escaping and touching the meat.

3. Roll the animal onto its back. This can be a challenge if you are alone or if the animal is on a slope. If the animal is on a slope and there is no way you can move it to level ground, then look for a nearby tree or bush on the uphill side of the animal. Tie off a length of rope on the uphill front leg; then tie the other end to the tree or bush, tightening the line to keep the animal on its back or as close as you can get. If you have a partner, have him or her steady the animal on its back while you straddle the animal facing to the animal's rear. If you put your right leg right behind the elk's leg to your right and your left leg in front of the elk's leg to your left, this further helps to stabilize the elk as you begin to work. If you are working alone, this same "sit astride" technique works about as well as any.

4. Make a shallow cut through the skin just below the breastbone. If you plan to cape the animal, ask your taxidermist how he prefers you to cut the cape and remove the hide. At the point of the initial cut, insert the index and center fingers of your other hand through the cut facing the elk's back end. Carefully insert the knife with the blade facing away from the body between these two fingers. The fingers form a guide for the blade as you begin to work it through the hide all the way to the back of the elk.

Note: If you are dressing out a bull, you may want to remove the genitals prior to making this cut. During the course of the run after being shot, bull elk often urinate on and by removing this part, you minimize the possibility of contaminating the meat with urine. To do this, just prior to the penis and sheath, direct your cut around the genitals to the left and to the right, coming together again near the cut you originally made to free the rectum. Now skin the entire penis and sheath from the animal all the way back to the testicles. Cut the muscles and tendons, pulling everything to the rear of the animal. Some states require that evidence of sex remain attached. If this is the case in the state in which you are hunting, be sure to leave either one testicle (bull) or some portion of the mammary gland (cow) attached to the abdominal wall. If your state does not require this, you can continue to remove the genitals all the way to the rear. Some minor cutting and tissue removal is required to accomplish this. Make sure that the hide is cut all the way to the pelvic bone.

5. Now that you have cut the hide and separated the genitals, go back to where you made the cut in the chest and make a second cut along the same path through the abdominal wall all the way to the rear. Be very careful that you do not cut too deep and puncture the paunch (gut). If you err and cut too deep, you will know almost immediately that you messed up, as you will be rewarded with a unique and almost overwhelming stench that you never knew existed as gut gasses begin to escape. Once this cut is complete all the way back to the pelvic bone, reach into the area below the pelvic bone and extract the tied-off rectum, pulling it back into the cavity.

6. To remove the viscera (guts), reach as far forward inside the body cavity as possible and cut the windpipe and esophagus. This can be a bit messy, but it has to be done.

7. Once you have cut the windpipe, the entire gut can be removed by using both hands to pull it away from the inside of the body cavity. You may have to

The meat is a delicacy—bull or cow.

Hunting in snow brings its own challenges—and so many rewards.

make one or two small cuts if something hangs up, but the internal organs should all come out at once with little effort.

8. Continue to drain as much blood from the cavity as possible.

9. The next step is to begin removing the hide. While there are a few advantages to leaving a hide on if you have to drag the carcass some distance, the disadvantages far outweigh any advantage. As soon as the animal dies, bacteria begins to form in the meat. Removing the hide allows the meat to cool faster, thus slowing the process of bacterial growth. By cooling the meat immediately, you are making every effort to preserve the quality of the meat. Unless you manage to kill your elk in camp or while it's standing in the bed of your pickup, you will want to quarter the animal for transport anyhow.

10. When skinning an elk, a good place to start is just above the center joint in the leg. Inserting your knife at this point just inside the leg, make a cut all the way to the chest. Then return to the point where you started and cut completely around the leg, cutting from inside the hide to outside. By cutting from inside to outside, you avoid getting hair on your meat and your knife stays sharp much longer since it isn't cutting through hair. Repeat this process for all four legs.

11. Once all four legs have been skinned, begin skinning the hide away from the body itself. I prefer to work my way from the original chest cavity cut, up toward the backbone, working on one side at a time. Once the entire hide on one side has been cut away, lay the hide, hair side down, on the ground away from the body; be sure not to get dirt on the exposed inner side of the hide. When the entire hide from one side has been skinned back to the backbone, you can begin the quartering process.

12. Quartering an elk is made easier with the use of a bone saw. There are any number of these made specifically for hunters, available at your local sporting goods store. After skinning one side of your elk, with it lying on its unskinned side, remove the head and all four legs. The head can be removed using your knife and saw just behind the ears. This leaves the maximum amount of neck meat remaining. With your saw, cut the legs off just below the joint where you began the skinning process. Next separate the front quarter from the rear quarter by making a cut behind the rib cage. As hindquarters are heavier than front quarters, think about how far forward you make this cut. The farther forward, the more the hindquarters weigh. Next, remove the quarters from the opposite half by cutting right down the center of the backbone with your saw. You now have two separate quarters on that side. Take each quarter and place it into a clean game bag. Now fold the clean hide that you carefully laid out back into its original position, roll the elk onto the side you just quartered and repeat the process for the opposite side.

13. Once you have removed and bagged all four quarters, don't forget to remove the tastiest parts—the backstraps and the tenderloin. Backstraps are located along either side of the top of the spine. When cut, they are long and triangular in shape. These should be carefully removed by making a longitudinal cut along each side of the spine, followed by a second cut beneath each strap. Next, look under the spine and, with your knife, remove the tenderloins, which lie in a similar location beneath the spine. These are a bit shorter in length and round in shape. As this is my favorite part of the elk, I usually place these cuts in a special bag all by themselves labeled "if the airplane catches fire, save these first."

14. Depending on your personal preference, you can now remove any additional rib, neck or other meat that you like.

The Gutless Method

Recently, many elk hunters have switched to what we are calling the gutless method of quartering an elk. Not only will this method save you time and effort, but it is also far less messy and you will not have to deal with the gut. Time required? About an hour.

The Steps
Here are the steps I use:

1. Roll the elk onto its side and position its feet heading downhill. If the animal is on a slope and you need to stabilize it, use the 50-feet (15 m) of cord to tie it off to a nearby tree or good-size rock.

2. Using your knife, make a cut through the hide from just behind the elk's skull down the spine all the way to the tail. Make another cut through the hide just behind the scapula (shoulder blade) around to the brisket.

3. Skin the shoulder. Some prefer to leave the hide on to keep out the dirt until putting the shoulder into a meat bag. I prefer to remove the hide as soon as possible to begin cooling the meat and slowing bacteria growth. Either way works; it's your call.

4. Lift the leg, remove the shoulder and place in a game bag. Remove as much rib and neck meat as you desire. This is where a fifth game bag comes in handy.

5. Skin the hindquarter on this side and remove by cutting against the pelvic bone until you reach the joint. Cut remaining tendons and ligaments and place in a game bag.

6. Remove the back straps by cutting down the spine from head to tail and peeling this piece away from the spine and upper ribs. Place in a game bag.

7. Remove the tenderloins (located inside the carcass on either side of the spine) by either cutting through the tops of the ribs or by pulling them free by reaching under the spine between the ribs. Place in a game bag.

8. Flip the animal over and repeat the process.

Boning Your Meat

If it is a long hike back to camp and you will have to haul the meat out on your back, consider boning your meat out before you pack it out. It may take you a bit more time, but boning the meat out can lighten your load by as much as 50 pounds (23 kg).

I prefer using heavy-duty cotton game bags as opposed to the lightweight cheesecloth-type bags often used for deer. A bull elk hindquarter can easily weigh 80 pounds (36 kg) or more and experience has taught me that these lightweight bags just don't hold up as well as a set of sturdy cotton game bags.

Hauling Your Meat

Well, you have had the fun part, experienced the messy part, and now the "less fun" part begins. That is hauling your elk back to camp. If you have boned the meat out, you can line your backpack with a regular large plastic trash bag, fill it with meat and begin your trek. If you have chosen to leave the bone in, securely lash a quarter to a good pack frame and start walking.

What if you have to leave your elk or some part of your elk in the field? To protect the bagged quarters from birds or other animals, I suggest hanging them from a limb in a cool spot in some trees. If there are no trees available, look for some logs or limbs to rest the bagged quarter over. This facilitates the cooling process while you are gone. Finally, some hunters have been known to urinate around the site to discourage bears, wolves or coyotes from coming near the meat.

INDEX

PHOTO CREDITS

Note: T = Top, B = Bottom, C = Center, L = left, R = Right, I = inset

© Andrew Bracken: pp. 14, 37, 70, 72, 96, 100, 102

© Jim Christensen: pp. 17, 19, 21, 22, 32, 39 (top), 41, 42, 44, 45 (both), 50, 55, 62, 65, Back Cover (bottom left)

© Davis Tent & Awning: p. 94 (left)

© Michael H. Francis: pp. 12, 49 (bottom)

© Jerry Gowins: pp. 15, 28, 31, 46, 71, 105, 107, 117

© Eric J. Hansen: pp.13, 30, 59 (right), 60 (left), 82 (right), 89

© Jay Houston: pp. 26 (left), 27, 59 (left), 67 (right), 69, Front Cover (inset), Back Cover (top left)

© iStock Images: pp. 6, 7, 25, 36 (top), 43, 48, 75 (top), 79 (bottom), 81, 82 (left), 91, 94 (right), Front Cover

© Brad Knutson: pp. 24, 64, 73, 79 (top)

© Gary Kramer/garykramer.net: pp. 26 (right), 60 (right)

© Lon E. Lauber: pp. 10, 11, 16, 18, 34 (bottom), 51, 52, 57, 58, 66, 67 (left), 68, 75 (bottom), 76, 80, 83, 84, 88, 90, 92, 93, 120, Back Cover (bottom right)

© Jeff McKinney: p. 118, 122, 123

© Mark Raycroft: pp. 4, 40 (bottom), 47, 86

© Jerry Taylor: pp. 8, 20, 33, 34 (top), 35 (both), 36 (bottom), 38, 39 (bottom), 40 (top), 49 (top), 54, 56, 61, 74, 78, 98, 106, 110, 112, 114, Back Cover (top right)

Creative Publishing international
Your Complete Source of How-to Information for the Outdoors

Hunting Books
* Advanced Turkey Hunting
* Advanced Whitetail Hunting
* Beginner's Guide to Birdwatching
* Black Bear Hunting
* Bowhunting Equipment & Skills
* Bowhunter's Guide to Accurate Shooting
* The Complete Guide to Hunting
* Dog Training
* How to Think Like a Survivor
* Hunting Record-Book Bucks
* Mule Deer Hunting
* Muzzleloading
* Outdoor Guide to Using Your GPS
* Waterfowl Hunting
* Whitetail Addicts Manual
* Whitetail Hunting
* Whitetail Techniques & Tactics
* Wild Turkey

Fishing Books
* Advanced Bass Fishing
* The Art of Freshwater Fishing
* Catching Panfish
* The Complete Guide to Freshwater Fishing
* Fishing for Catfish
* Fishing Tips & Tricks
* Fishing with Artificial Lures
* Inshore Salt Water Fishing
* Kids Gone Campin'
* Kids Gone Fishin'
* Kids Gone Paddlin'
* Largemouth Bass
* Live Bait Fishing
* Modern Methods of Ice Fishing
* Northern Pike & Muskie
* Salt Water Fishing Tactics
* Smallmouth Bass
* Striped Bass Fishing: Salt Water Strategies
* Successful Walleye Fishing
* Ultralight Fishing
* Trout

Fly Fishing Books
* The Art of Fly Tying + CD-ROM
* Complete Photo Guide to Fly Fishing
* Complete Photo Guide to Fly Tying
* Fishing Dry Flies
* Fly-Fishing Equipment & Skills
* Fly Fishing for Beginners
* Fly Fishing for Trout in Streams
* Fly-Tying Techniques & Patterns

Cookbooks
* All-Time Favorite Game Bird Recipes
* America's Favorite Fish Recipes
* America's Favorite Wild Game Recipes
* Backyard Grilling
* Cooking Wild in Kate's Kitchen
* Dressing & Cooking Wild Game
* The New Cleaning & Cooking Fish
* Preparing Fish & Wild Game
* Venison Cookery
* The Wild Butcher
* The Wild Fish Cookbook
* The Wild Game Cookbook

To purchase these or other Creative Publishing international titles,
contact your local bookseller, or visit our website at
www.creativepub.com

  *The Complete*
FLY FISHERMAN™